Potomac Street Irregulars

THE

PROCEEDINGS OF THE

Potomac Street Irregulars

A Study Group of Antietam Historical Association

VOLUME I

EDITED BY

TODD ANDREW DORSETT.

"Nothing clears up a case so much as stating it to another person."

—SIR ARTHUR CONAN DOYLE

WAYNESBORO, PENNSYLVANIA
MMXIV

Published in 2014 by
Antietam Historical Association
119 West Main Street
Waynesboro, Pennsylvania 17268

ISBN 978-0-9909864-0-9

Library of Congress Control Number : 2014919252

Printed and bound in the United States of America
Mercersburg Printing, Inc.

Design and typography by T. A. Dorsett.

Preface.

OR nearly two years, the Potomac Street Irregulars have studied crime in the Antietam country of Maryland and Pennsylvania and contiguous regions. Typically one member, called the "lead detective," will research an historic case and then present his findings to the group during a meeting. Thereupon, the assemblage as a whole analyzes the case, sometimes hoping to solve mysteries. These proceedings attract a broad spectrum of citizens, from teenagers to nonagenarians; and because they pursue their mission lightheartedly, this unlikely collection of students has become a cohesive group of amateur sleuths and friends.

The undersigned conceived the Potomac Street Irregulars after reading some of Sir Arthur Conan Doyle's detective stories, wherein Sherlock Holmes employs a band of street urchins, led by the redoubtable Wiggins, to gather information for use in solving crimes. Holmes christened those children the "Baker Street Irregulars," and paid them for their services. While not compensated with money for their work, the Potomac Street Irregulars are nonetheless effective in gathering from the repositories of historical records the facts of the cases they seek to explain or solve. Enlightenment and fellowship are their remuneration.

The Potomac Street Irregulars operate under the auspices of Antietam Historical Association, whose mission is processing information about the region in Maryland and Pennsylvania drained by Antietam creek. While not abandoning scholarship, Antietam Historical Association often engages in lighthearted or even humorous activities in order to maintain a broad base of engagement. In keeping with this tongue-in-cheek approach to History, the Potomac Street Irregulars' nickname, "PSI," is a parody of the titles of certain television crime dramas.

To launch the Potomac Street Irregulars, fifteen persons met at The Waynesburger, situated at the corner of West Main street

and South Potomac avenue, Waynesboro, Pennsylvania, on Tuesday, January 8, 2013. They resolved to assemble on the second
Tuesday of every month at some restaurant located along the
route called "Potomac" which passes through Waynesboro and
the Maryland cities of Hagerstown and Sharpsburg on its way to
the Potomac river. The second meeting and all other subsequent
gatherings but one have occurred at the Parlor House, Waynesboro.

The original Potomac Street Irregulars were the Misses Sue
Stoner and Shirley A. Zeigler, Mesdames Jody Henke, F. M. Rock
(president of Antietam Historical Association), and Darlene S.
Weddle, Mr. and Mrs. Frank Bock, Mr. and Mrs. J. Michael Logan, Mr. and Mrs. Harry G. Morningstar, and Messrs. L. Dean
Calimer, T. A. Dorsett, Franklin J. Shockey, and Timothy J.
Shockey. Little did these pioneer Irregulars realize that, in a few
months' time, their numbers would swell to more than eighty
persons, with attendance sometimes exceeding the recommended capacity of the meeting room.

Because the group's rules forbid discussing cases involving living persons, and because one cannot defame the dead, PSI dis-
cussions can be as candid or as speculative as the members wish.
Because most of the investigated crimes occurred many decades
ago, this frank exchange of ideas is unlikely to offend anyone,
for today even the families of perpetrators and victims alike are
intellectually curious about these historic incidents. The Irregulars can therefore view each case objectively and thus produce
reliable results.

The present volume represents the first year's work of the Potomac Street Irregulars. Publishing these proceedings will serve
several purposes. First, it will preserve the conscientious efforts
of the lead detectives. Second, it will share the PSI product with
those who cannot attend the actual meetings. And, third, it will
help to promote a better understanding of the group itself.

In the present compilation, cases are set forth in the order in
which the Irregulars discussed them. Under the title of each investigation appear both the name of its lead detective and the
date of his presentation. Whenever available, the speaker's

narrative is used as the chapter text; otherwise, the Editor has needed to substitute his own statement of the case. The Editor thanks the following "lead detectives" for submitting material for this publication: Mrs. Sue Shockey Lee and Messrs. Frank Bock and Franklin J. Shockey. Mr. Shockey, as well as Messrs. Scott K. Parker and Timothy J. Shockey, have also rendered valuable technical services in conducting and recording the PSI meetings. Numerous other persons have helped the Irregulars gather facts and images pertaining to the crimes set forth in this volume, and receive due credit within the recitation of the case in which they are interested or in credits accompanying the images they provided.

Each PSI lead detective chooses his own presentation format. Some elect straightforward speeches; some use engaging "props"; others create digitally illustrated lectures. Consequently, in order for this volume to have some aspect of consistency while still providing the reader with the full effect of each investigation, it has been necessary to convert each of these cases into a common format.

Antietam Historical Association cannot deny that the PSI mission appeals to mankind's baser instincts. For whatever reason, crime and punishment excite ready interest in a cross section of any community. But if, by studying the seamy side of life, the group's members become more enlightened about what causes people to misbehave and how society can react to crime more thoughtfully and productively, then the supreme purpose of History—a better world—is served.

TODD ANDREW DORSETT.

Waynesboro, Pennsylvania,
October 31, 2014.

Contents.

Illustrations.

Arthur Conan Doyle.

Introduction.

CRIME is "an act committed or omitted in violation of a law forbidding or commanding it."* It has existed throughout history; for unless a statute has the unanimous support of the people subject to it, there will be those who disregard it. At the same time, there are citizens who unwittingly violate the law, yet "ignorance of the law excuses no one." Therefore, absent a legitimate defense, both knowing and unknowing violators are perpetrators of what we know as "crime."

When determining what constitutes "crime," most cultures begin by promulgating laws vindicating the ruling authority. Next, they outlaw actions causing personal harm. Consequently, in English-speaking nations, the traditional felonies were treason, murder, burglary, arson, rape, robbery, kidnapping, and sodomy. Over the years, however, lawmakers have expanded the body of the criminal law to include a multiplicity of offenses too numerous to mention here, while only a handful of "crimes" have been legalized. So crime is always with us, and this reality provides the Potomac Street Irregulars with an almost inexhaustible amount of grist for their investigative mill.

Fast on the heels of Crime flies Punishment. It takes many forms, and changes with the evolving tastes and beliefs of the community. For centuries, superstitious, self-righteous authorities inflicted unspeakable misery upon their fellow men when presuming to punish them; for instance, until the Nineteenth century, the aforementioned felonies were typically capital crimes, and in some countries they remain so. On the other hand, there are thinkers who believe that it is not the prerogative of one man to punish another. As self-governance and education have

---

*William Morris, ed., *The American Heritage Dictionary of the English Language* (Boston: Houghton Mifflin Company, 1979), p. 313.

become more widespread, pragmatic legislators have sought a compromise between these two opposing reactions to crime. As a result of this process, harsh penalties have become less prevalent. After all, a well-informed, self-governing citizenry knows that prosecution for a criminal offense, howsoever petty, can visit anyone's doorstep. As part of that movement, Pennsylvania was the second State to limit capital punishment to murder cases.

When the Age of Enlightenment produced the United States of America, the Founding Fathers defied conservative practices, declaring in the Eighth Amendment to the Constitution, "Excessive bail shall not be required, nor excessive fines imposed, nor cruel and unusual punishments inflicted." Their vision has produced a longstanding trend towards a more reasoned approach to crime and punishment in America.

Whipping-posts were a means of punishment for crime in some States into the Twentieth century.

Accordingly, the Potomac Street Irregulars' investigations have run the gamut from an Eighteenth-century case where Pennsylvania hanged a man merely for uttering counterfeit money, to Twentieth-century cases where courts have shown mercy on an array of guilty defendants. And it is important to note that these two extremes in punishment proved equally effective deterrents against continued criminal conduct.

A century ago, Clarence Darrow noted that "mercy is the highest attribute of man." He realized that no one makes a conscious decision "to be bad"; on the contrary, something in nature makes each individual feel differently, think differently, and behave differently than other persons. At the same time, the law must protect society. One of the goals of the Potomac Street Irregulars, therefore, is to encourage people to ponder both crime and punishment more scientifically, with an eye to a better understanding of the human condition. How might we maintain order without wronging the perceived wrongdoer?

The country in Maryland and Pennsylvania drained by Antietam creek, as well as the circumjacent territory, has proved a fertile venue for crime. Between 1863, when the State of West Virginia was created, and 1912, when Arizona and New Mexico were admitted into the Union, the Antietam watershed claimed the only spot where one could view four States simultaneously. A desperado would consider this circumstance advantageous for escape from one jurisdiction to another. Consequently, the region where Maryland, Pennsylvania, Virginia, and West Virginia nearly converge was traditionally a place of refuge for men "on the lam." This was especially true before and during the Civil War, when this locality served as a buffer zone between the two principal "sections" of an uneasy nation. The environs of the towns of Bolivar and Harper's Ferry, West Virginia, being almost surrounded by rugged mountains and treacherous waterways, yet within close reach of three of the aforementioned States, were a particular place of resort for rogues of yesteryear.

One can easily imagine that the lonely sylvan features of the South Mountain, where both branches of Antietam rise, could lull a mischievous person into believing he could perpetrate a crime there without being detected. This was particularly true in the days when the population was more concentrated in valley towns and villages. Historically, the people who inhabited the mountains and their rims were a fiercely independent folk, some of whom seemed strongly inclined towards violence and subterfuge. This combination of scenery and actors made the South Mountain the perfect setting for a variety of crimes. Indeed, the murders of Emanuel Monn, Jacob Shockey, Samuel Shockey, and the Newey household all occurred within its wooded precincts. In early times, counterfeiter Valentine Shockey and his cohort sought refuge in the mountain fastnesses when pursued by the authorities. And the attack on Miss Betty Jane Kennedy, if not committed in the hills, at least resulted in her dying there.

The towns and countryside of the Cumberland Valley have also hosted their share of crime. Some persons have been so desperate that they committed violent crimes in densely populated settings. John Monn and John Lesher both killed their wives in

downtown Waynesboro, Pennsylvania, residences, with no hope
of evading detection, and William Reed strolled through Mont
Alto, Pennsylvania, after shooting his former sweetheart in one
of the buildings of the forestry school nearby.

Sometimes the Antietam country was merely part of a larger
territory in which a crime spree occurred. The local counterfeiters of the Eighteenth century belonged to a network of outlaws
who operated throughout the Middle Atlantic colonies. Meantime, the adventures of David Lewis and Gerard R. Peabody kept
both bandits traversing South Mountain, the great valley, and
regions far beyond the scope of the Potomac Street Irregulars.
What, then, is the correlation, if any, between setting and crime?

While studying historic crimes, the Potomac Street Irregulars
have recognized some popular misapprehensions. Is the Twen-
ty-first-century world more violent than it was previously? The
frequency and ferocity of Nineteenth- and Twentieth-century
crimes committed hereabouts suggest that, if anything, today's
world is perhaps a little *less* violent. The early-Twentieth-centu-
ry Monn and Lesher domestic killings in Waynesboro, the 1829
Newey massacre near Sabillasville, Maryland, and the Eighteenth-century execution of Christopher Shockey in Cumberland county, Pennsylvania, clearly demonstrate the cruelty and
violence of olden times.

Another widely accepted fallacy is that modern criminal courts
are "softer on crime" than were the tribunals of a century or more
ago. While it is true that old-time capital and corporal punishments are either abolished or less readily employed, the Potomac
Street Irregulars have learnt that juries in the Nineteenth and
early Twentieth centuries often sympathized with guilty defendants, finding them either not guilty or at least guilty of lesser offenses than their prosecutors had preferred. A prime example of
this phenomenon is the case of John Lesher, of Waynesboro, who
shot and killed his wife. The evidence clearly showed that Lesher intended to shoot his wife, and that he admittedly fired at her
twice before nonchalantly leaving her to die. At the same time,
the evidence also showed that Lesher was a reputable man; that
he probably acted under the influence of defective bootleg whis-

key, and that Mrs. Lesher had the reputation of a wild and unfaithful woman. So, rather than convicting Lesher of first-degree murder, of which he stood accused, the jury found him guilty of a lesser offense. Their verdict thus precluded a sentence of death and perhaps granted Lesher the opportunity to mate peacefully with a more reputable woman.

Why are guilty parties sometimes undetected? The sensational murder case arising from the brutal slaying of Miss Betty Jane Kennedy, of Hagerstown, Maryland, is an example of an unsolved case. Beginning in 1946, numerous law enforcement agencies have investigated that homicide but none has ever charged anyone as the perpetrator of that famous crime. Perhaps the simultaneous involvement of so many lawmen from different jurisdictions is precisely why they have never resolved the matter. Perhaps the explanation is more esoteric. Howbeit, in the hope of solving that murder case, the Potomac Street Irregulars have determined to revisit its investigation on an annual basis beginning in April 2015.

Miss Kennedy's case also illustrates how crime victims often recklessly expose themselves to danger. On the evening when Miss Kennedy left her familial abode for the last time, she disregarded her sister's admonition to be more careful, and exited to her doom. Similarly, when John Monn, of Waynesboro, was charged with viciously assaulting his wife, Mrs. Monn failed to testify against him. Monn was duly discharged, and the couple resumed their cohabitation. Within several years, however, Monn killed his wife. Thus, self-victimization poses another question for the Potomac Street Irregulars: To what extent shall society protect those who throw caution to the wind?

Is the government sometimes uninterested in pursuing the perpetrators of crimes? The 1928 murder of Samuel Shockey, an escapee from Pennsylvania's Eastern Penitentiary, suggests an affirmative answer. Shockey had led a lawless life, was convicted of killing his

Decapitation has been a popular form of capital punishment throughout history.

The pillory was another ancient form of punishment which brought out the worst in the community.

equally wayward brother Jacob, and was found murdered in the mountains where he had been hiding. A thorough investigation undertaken by Shockey's grandnephew suggests that the murder remains unsolved largely because the Commonwealth of Pennsylvania viewed Shockey's death as a positive development in crime-fighting.

At least two PSI cases demonstrate the folly of labelling and compartmentalizing human behaviour into absolutes. Schoolmaster David Lewis, known as the "Robin Hood of Pennsylvania" as well as "the terror of the Cumberland Valley," was a threat only to the "haves" and their lackeys; he was a dashing, kindly hero to many "have nots." The likable Gerard R. Peabody, gentleman bank robber and sometime radio technician, never harmed anyone during his heists; he just seems to have enjoyed robbing banks. He wilfully and repeatedly engaged in conduct which ultimately placed him on Alcatraz Island when he could have been enjoying a princely inheritance. Both of these criminals were obviously in some degree sociopathic, but both of their cases also support the belief that no one is either entirely virtuous or entirely evil. What, then, causes otherwise admirable citizens to embrace lives of crime?

Often crime has a humorous aspect. This is particularly true when a perpetrator bungles his crime, but even the most dreadful situation may conjure hilarious images in the playful mind. If one embraces a detached, scientific approach to studying crime, he can laugh at the foibles of wrongdoers and victims alike without losing sight of his mission. The testimony of trial witnesses can also provoke laughter. For instance, when asked what an "insane man" was, one prosecution witness in the murder trial of John D. Lesher replied that he had seen that kind of person in insane asylums!

On the other hand, becoming mired in righteous indignation or moroseness can fatally flaw an historical investigation. Fortunately, the Potomac Street Irregulars good-naturedly confront all of the questions posed above. This pleasant and unrestrained approach to studying crime has provided a likely solution to at least one unsolved murder case, and has resulted in meaningful progress on another. It entertains while educating a remarkable cross-section of the community. It provides a clearer understanding of earlier lifestyles. Consequently it should serve, though in ever so small proportion, to guide mankind along a better path.

Nescire autem quid ante quam natus sis acciderit, id est semper esse puerum.
—Cicero.

I.

The Murder of Emanuel Monn.

TODD ANDREW DORSETT.

January 8, 2013.

The inaugural meeting of the Potomac Street Irregulars was held at The Waynes-burger, Waynesboro. Fifteen persons attended. The agenda included a summary discussion of the late-Nineteenth-century murder of Emanuel Monn.

*F*INDINGS of guilt based entirely upon circumstantial evidence often provoke lively debate about the soundness of verdicts, particularly in cases resulting in executions. The conviction and hanging of Henry Heist for the murder of Emanuel Monn was one such case. More than a century afterwards, people in Adams and Franklin counties, Pennsylvania, still hold strong opinions as to whether Heist was guilty of murdering Monn; and if one believes that Heist was innocent of that crime, then one typically can name the other person or persons on whom suspicion should linger.

Henry Heist and Emanuel Monn were reared in the "Black Corner," at the western foot of Curve Mountain in the vicinity of the present Biesecker's Gap and Glen Forney. They were woodchoppers, and Heist employed young Monn in that capacity while working on the opposite slope of South Mountain, near Maria Furnace, Adams county. The twain inhabited a log shanty erected near their work site, and there the murder is supposed to have occurred on or about February 2, 1893.

At the time of the murder, Heist was approximately twenty-eight years old and recently released from Pennsylvania's Eastern Penitentiary, Philadelphia. He was described as tall and muscular. Monn was around nineteen years of age. Heist referred to him either as "the boy" or "Big Feet."

On February 1, 1893, Heist and Monn attended a party at the

residence of George Reese, which was the nearest dwelling to their shanty. Reese was married to Heist's half-sister, Anna Rebecca Hollinger, who had previously been married to J. Cooper McCleaf. Both Heist and Monn were enamored of Mrs. Reese's daughter Susan McCleaf, aged about seventeen years at the time. Susan, it appears, preferred Emanuel Monn, and made plans with him to visit relatives in Franklin county within the next few days. That was the last time anyone (except the killer) saw Monn alive.

When the time arrived for Emanuel Monn to meet Miss McCleaf, Henry Heist appeared at the Reese place instead. When asked where Emanuel was, Heist indicated that the boy had already gone to his home. So Susan and Henry travelled over the mountain together. When Emanuel's family inquired about him, Heist made the contradictory statement that Monn had gone to Gettysburg and Seven Stars, Adams county, to work, and rebuked Susan when she mentioned that she had believed Emanuel to be at his home.[1]

After Heist's statements made them suspicious, the Monn family raised the alarm that Emanuel was missing. A search ensued but was hampered by the harsh winter weather. On March 12 the search party was in the close proximity of Heist's shanty when Christian C. Shockey, of Franklin county, noticed an odd jumble of rocks, rails, and brush with a tree trunk placed on top of it. He and some other searchers went to the site, some two hundred eighteen feet across a ravine from the shanty. When the men removed the top layers of the pile, a boot was seen protruding from below, and the body of Emanuel Monn was found in a shallow grave underneath the stones.[2]

Monn's body was well preserved, largely because of the cold weather. The scene and corpse were photographed, and a physician was summoned to examine the body in the makeshift grave.

---

[1] "Heist Found Guilty," *Gettysburg Compiler* (Gettysburg, Pa.), September 5, 1893, p. 3.

[2] "On Trial for Murder," *The Times* (Philadelphia, Pa.), August 29, 1893, p. 3. *See also* "Convicted of a Horrible Murder," Reading Times (Reading, Pa.), September 4, 1893, p. 1; "Murder in the First Degree," *The Times*, September 3, 1893, p. 4, and "Heist Found Guilty," *supra*.

Dr. A. O. Scott examined Monn's body at the grave. He later testified that he first saw the body lying in a large trench:—

"I found a cut in the throat, the skull crushed in the forehead and a wound back of the left ear. The wound back of the left ear was a large one and seemed as if it had been made by a succession of blows. The wound in the forehead was apparently made by a hatchet or hammer. The wound in the throat was about 3½ inches long and was deep enough to almost reach the bone. The wind pipe was severed and a part of the chin cut away. This wound was done by one blow."

Cross-examination of Dr. Scott produced this testimony:—

"I examined the body partly in the grave and partly out. The body was lying on its back. The wound behind the right ear was deep enough to reach the bone. The skin was cut. The diameter of this wound was about ½ inch but I don't think the skull back of the right ear was fractured. The body was exposed sometime before I got there. The body, from its appearance, may have been in the grave for a month or more. This wound might have been made on a dead body. The wound was slightly curved and was not cut with a sharp instrument. The wound on the forehead was of an inch in diameter with an indentation of about one-sixteenth of an inch. There might have been another injury other than these which I have described that might have caused death. Either the wound on the forehead, behind left ear, or the one in the throat would have been fatal. The wound in the throat was about the size of one made by a sharp hatchet, and must have been made while lying down with the head thrown back."

Dr. James E. Glenn also examined the body:—

"I noted on the forehead of the dead man a wound and the bone was broken. There was a wound behind the left ear in which I pressed my little finger at least 1¼ inches through the skull into the brain. There was a cut in the throat with a part of the chin chipped away. The wounds on the forehead, back of both right and left ears were made by a blunt instrument. The wound on the forehead looked very much as if it had been made by this hatchet (held one without a handle in his hands). The wound behind the left ear would have been necessarily fatal."

On cross-examination, Dr. Glenn explained,—

> "I was not there to make a post mortem examination but merely out of curiosity as others were. I cannot say whether the wounds were made before or after death. I did not lift the head to make a careful examination of the wounds on the back of the head. There is a difference between wounds made on a dead or living body. The wound extended to almost the angle of the jaw. The head must have been thrown back when that wound was made."[3]

Suspicion had already fixed on Heist, who was roaming about the country along the base of the mountain, between Old Forge and Greenwood. At the residences of John Henry Barnes and Jacob Monn, he complained of suffering in his head, and was at one point placed under a physician's care.

On March 18, 1893, after spending the night in the barn of one Scott between Chambersburg and Gettysburg, the beleaguered Heist, in company with Scott's son Harvey, appeared at the Adams county sheriff's office. The sheriff was summoned, and Heist was taken into custody and placed in the granite cell of the county jail. Several days later, Heist told newspaper reporters that he was innocent; that Monn had gone to Gettysburg to buy a coat and vest, intending to be gone two weeks; that Miss Susan McCleaf had accompanied him to Monn's father's house, and that, meantime, he had heard about Monn's death, and so remained in the vicinity. He was determined that Constable Samuel Rock, who had apprehended him previously, should not arrest him again.[4] He also claimed that he and Monn had never had any difficulty between them, and that he liked Monn. Heist stated that Monn had mentioned travelling to Frederick, Maryland.[5]

Whether he was guilty or not guilty, the cards were stacked against Heist. He was well known in Adams and Franklin counties as a chicken thief and all-around "bad man." Regional news-

HEIST'S SHANTY.

---

[3] "Heist Found Guilty," *supra.*

[4] *Gettysburg Compiler*, March 21, 1893, p. 3.

[5] "The Monn Murder Mystery," *The Daily News* (Mount Carmel, Pa.), March 20, 1893, p. 2.

HENRY HEIST,
From a photograph made the day of his execution.

papers recounted his sordid history, some of which they had obtained from hearsay, so the news had probably prejudiced prospective jurors even before Heist was taken into custody. Additionally, whenever asked questions about Monn's whereabouts, Heist gave contradictory replies. And, finally, there was testimony that Heist behaved brutally even when he knew he was already suspected of murder. Nancy Monn, sister of Emanuel, testified at the trial to this effect:—

"I know Heist. Heist and Susan McCleaf came to our house on February third. Susie asked if [Emanuel] was home. Heist said she knew very well that he was not coming home. He had gone to Gettysburg and from there to Seven Stars. Heist wanted Susie to go away with him. When she refused he threw her across the room and struck her. I next saw Heist on Friday the 17th. He had a flour bag with him. He put it down and said none of the kids should touch it. He came back in about two weeks and complained of his head. He was there the day [Emanuel's] body was found. He had a big club in his hand, and asked me what the people were doing out there. One day Clara Monn said she wished Emanuel would come home. Heist replied that if one was away a few days she thought him dead and buried."

She continued under cross-examination: "I saw Heist on the Monday before the murder and asked him when he was coming over. He said on Friday or Saturday. Heist was at our house four times between the 1st of February and March 17th."[6]

All of the evidence in the case suggested that Heist had murdered Monn. He certainly had more opportunity to accomplish

---

[6] "Heist Found Guilty," *supra.*

that feat than anyone else: he and Monn dwelt together in close quarters. The prosecution assumed that Heist's jealousy over Susan McCleaf was his motive. But there was no shred of direct evidence that Heist killed Monn.

Heist had a steady history of thieving. In 1885, Adams county prosecuted Heist and George Reese on five counts of larceny. His co-defendant in that matter was the same man whom Heist would ultimately accuse of murdering Emanuel Monn.

In 1887, Adams county prosecuted Heist for stealing a turkey, but he was acquitted.[7] In the same year, however, a Franklin county jury convicted him of larceny, and the court sentenced Heist to serve two years and ten months in the penitentiary. His aunt's husband, John Henry Barnes, was also convicted in that matter but was not sentenced with Heist.[8]

In 1891, "Hen" Heist was again in Franklin County Court charged with larceny. He was found guilty of stealing thirteen chickens from Jeremiah Shockey. The court considered Heist's previous conviction in sentencing him to pay a fine of five dollars and to serve fifteen months of solitary confinement in Eastern Penitentiary.[9]

In May 1893, the Adams county grand jury found a true bill against Heist for larceny and receiving stolen property on information of James Watson. The murder case was pending, however, so the larceny case was continued.[10]

The trial of Henry Heist for the murder of Emanuel Monn opened on Tuesday, August 29, 1893. The Commonwealth's theory in prosecuting Heist for the murder of Emanuel Monn was that Heist was jealous of the attachment between Susan McCleaf and Monn, and that he killed the latter to remove him from the competition for Susan's affections.

Upwards of forty witnesses testified during the five-day trial. They included a surveyor, a photographer, physicians, Susan McCleaf, other relatives of Heist's and hers, friends and relatives of

---

[7] *Gettysburg Compiler*, January 25, 1887, p. 3.

[8] "Court Doings," *The Village Record* (Waynesboro, Pa.), December 15, 1887, p. 2, col. 3.

[9] "Court Proceedings," *The Village Record*, March 5, 1891, p. 2, col. 4.

[10] *Gettysburg Compiler*, May 2, 1893, p. 3.

Monn's, members of the search party, and policemen.[11]

On September 2, 1893, the jury found Henry Heist guilty of murder in the first degree.[12] On the twentieth, the court refused Heist's motion for a new trial and sentenced him to death.[13] The execution was scheduled for December 14. On December 5, however, Heist accused George Reese of killing Emanuel Monn, and described in gruesome detail how he had assisted Reese with the burial. Consequently, on December 8, Governor Robert E. Pattison granted Heist a reprieve until January 17, 1894.

The accusation against George Reese produced no arrest. On January 5, 1894, the Pennsylvania Board of Pardons denied a commutation of Heist's sentence to life imprisonment, and the execution occurred January 17 in the yard of the Adams County Jail.[14]

Heist met his death calmly but protested his innocence to the end. For their kindness towards him, Heist thanked the sheriffs who had had him in their care, and was even persuaded to forgive the district attorney whom he had considered his bitterest enemy. His last words were "I die an innocent man." At 11:15 A.M. the sheriff withdrew from the scaffold, the trap was sprung, and Heist plunged downward five feet. At 11:30 A.M. he was pronounced dead from strangulation.[15]

No one claimed Heist's body. His aunt and her husband, John Henry Barnes, were present inside the jail but declined responsibility for the corpse. Allegedly, Heist's parents had moved to Virginia during the pendency of his trial, and had changed their names to avoid association with the affair. His body was therefore buried in the graveyard affiliated with the old Adams County Almshouse, where a simple tablet marks his grave thus—

---

[11] "Heist Found Guilty," *supra.*

[12] "Murder in the First Degree," *supra.*

[13] "Sentenced to Death," *The Times*, September 21, 1893, p. 1.

[14] "Collins and Reinecker Go to Chair at Rockview Without Flinching," *The Gettysburg Times* (Gettysburg, Pa.), April 25, 1921, pp. 1, 4.

[15] "Heist Hanged," *Harrisburg Telegraph* (Harrisburg, Pa.), January 17, 1894, p. 1, col. 9.

HENRY HEIST
Died Jan 17, 1894
Aged 29 Yrs.

Originally, the word "hung" had been inscribed below Heist's age
on the tombstone, but has since been obliterated. There is now a
slight, irregular depression where once the label of Henry Heist's
ignominious fate was carved.

LAST WILL AND TESTAMENT OF HENRY HEIST,
Made at Gettysburg on January 16, 1894, the day prior to his execution.

II.
The Murders of Jacob and Samuel Shockey.

FRANKLIN J. SHOCKEY.

February 12, 2013.

The second meeting of the Potomac Street Irregulars was held at the Parlor House restaurant, Waynesboro. Nineteen persons attended. The lead detective, PSI Franklin "Jim" Shockey, has made an exhaustive investigation into the nineteen-twenties shooting of his great-uncle Jacob Shockey and the mysterious killing of his great-uncle Samuel Shockey in the woods of the South Mountain four years later. What follows are merely the highlights of his research.

O N March 20, 1924, Miss Iva Wills, Miss Catherine Woodring, and "Sam" Shockey were walking along a mountain trail at the west end of Beartown in southeastern Franklin county, Pennsylvania. One can only imagine the trio's conversation. Whatever it was, Sam's brother Jacob Shockey interrupted it when he met them at the fork in the road. Depending upon whom you believe, "Jake" was also either the husband or boyfriend of Iva Wills.[1] Seeing his wife, or girlfriend, with his broth-

---

[1] Iva Wills was born Iva Leggee on December 28, 1903, at Huntington, Cabell county, W. Va. She was a daughter of Henry H. Leggee and his wife, *nee* Maggie Dora Wills. When her parents divorced, Iva apparently moved across the Ohio river with her mother to Lawrence county, O., and assumed her mother's maiden name. On October 23, 1919, because of delinquency, she was admitted to the Ohio Girls' Industrial School at Delaware, O. (*Register of Girls Received and Paroled*, 1916-1944, *Volume* 3, *page* 30, *number* 6011). Sometime after her release from the Industrial School, Iva travelled with Jacob Shockey to his Beartown home under the guise of being his wife but later denied being married to him. After Shockey's death, Iva claimed she had accompanied him to Beartown relying on the *promise* of marriage. Following her release from jail, she resided briefly with a family at Lemoyne, Pa., but wished to return to Columbus. She left Pennsylvania early in June 1925. ["Iva Wills Has Gone to Ohio," *The Record-Herald* (Waynesboro, Pa.), June 3, 1925, p. 1, col. 2]. Shortly after returning to Ohio, she married Charles Llewellyn Thoman (1901–1935), a poolroom clerk who lies buried in Crawford county, O., but was divorced from him. For the remainder of her active career she worked as a waitress. In 1959 she was thus employed at Columbus's Tuck Inn restaurant. She died from natural causes at Columbus on

er Sam, combined with the liquor he had been drinking, pushed Jake—an already dangerous man—to the brink of murder.[2]

To some persons, what happened that day was no surprise. Jake had been searching for Iva throughout the settlement. Several times during his quest, he had threatened to shoot people. When one person told him Iva was at his brother Christian's house, Jake replied, "'Chris' is another one I will shoot." He had also threatened his brother Elmer and a Waynesboro tinsmith.

Jacob Shockey had a checkered history. Iva Wills had met him while he was serving in the 14th U. S. Infantry at Columbus, Ohio. He later deserted that unit, and after an interlude he enlisted in the 11th U. S. Cavalry at Columbus. After his military service, he worked for a year as a Michigan State Policeman (allegedly because he had such a good understanding of the criminal mind).[3] After returning to Beartown in March 1924, he worked at odd jobs.

So the residents of Beartown were not shocked when they heard that Jacob Shockey had stepped into the trio's path with a gun. Iva Wills would later tell investigators that the brothers had quarreled when Sam learned that Jake had slapped Iva a few weeks previous. Although both the brothers were armed when they met on the trail, they at first had a fist fight. They separated, and both were walking away when Jacob turned and fired his rifle at Sam, missing him. Sam then fired at Jacob, inflicting a fatal wound to Jacob's back.[4] After Sam covered Jake's body with brush, Iva and Sam fled into the mountains.

March 5, 1980. Her body was given to the anatomical department of the Ohio State University. Mr. Russ Pollitt, Genealogy Subject Specialist at Columbus (O.) Metropolitan Library, kindly provided research assistance in the quest for information on Iva Wills.—*Ed.*

[2] Jacob Emile Shockey (1895–1924) and Samuel Thomas Shockey (1899–1928) were sons of Jacob Henry Shockey and his first wife, *nee* Mary Catharine Reesman. Their brother Christian David (*alias* C. C.) Shockey (1891–1967) was the grandfather of PSI Franklin Shockey. Their brother Elmer H. Shockey (1888–1974) was the grandfather of Mr. Richard S. Shockey, of Beartown, among others.—*Ed.*

[3] *The Record-Herald*, March 22, 1924, p. 1, col. 7.

[4] The official report on the death of Jacob E. Shockey states that he died as the result of a "Gunshot wound on back of left shoulder, shot gun. Sudden death from hemorrhage of vessels from heart by unknown person" (Commonwealth of Pennsylvania Certificate of Death #25344).

Later, the boys' older brother Elmer Shockey discovered Jacob's body under the brush. Catherine Woodring then told of the fight the brothers had had, and the manhunt was on.

Meanwhile, the body of Jacob Shockey was removed to the funeral home of Frank E. Grove, South Church street, Waynesboro, where the autopsy was performed and an inquest held. Later, hundreds of curious citizens mobbed the funeral home for a glimpse of the murdered man. Two hundred persons attended the funeral at Calvary Episcopal Church, Beartown, and Jacob's remains were laid to rest in the adjoining graveyard.[5]

Authorities had been hunting Samuel Shockey for some time regarding a forgery charge preferred at Waynesboro, but after the shooting the search intensified. Sam had been hiding; now he was running. The posse, led by the State Police, walked quietly through a five-inch snowfall. Fearing that Sam's brother Elmer might try to warn Sam of their approach, the police carried their guns limbered as a warning to Elmer against any unnecessary noise. The police located Iva and Sam's homemade shelter in the mountains near the Adams county line, and surprised the two fugitives while they were cooking dinner.[6]

When thrown to the dirt floor of his hiding place, Sam calmly said, "I didn't think you men would be out in this weather."

At the county jail, Sam confessed to shooting Jake, claiming self-defense. The police countered that that was unlikely because Jacob had been shot in the back. Furthermore, a second autopsy revealed that Jake had also been hit in the head, not hard enough to kill him but enough to cause a concussion.[7]

---

[5] *The Evening News* (Harrisburg, Pa.), March 25, 1924, p. 15.

[6] "Brother and Wife of Victim Held in Mountain Slaying," *The Gettysburg Times* (Gettysburg, Pa.), March 22, 1924, p. 1. *See also* "Find Brother of Murdered Man in Mountain Region," *Harrisburg Telegraph* (Harrisburg, Pa.), March 21, 1924, p. 1.

[7] *Ibid.* At the time of the incident, Iva Wills was indicted as an accessory to the killing. Verily, the only contemporary published image of the red-haired *femme fatale* was a newspaper photograph of a smiling Iva holding a firearm. PSI Jim Shockey's considered opinion is that Sam Shockey confessed to shooting his brother in order to protect Iva from being convicted. He bases his conclusion on the fact that Jake was indeed shot from behind, while it was reported that after Jake and Sam separated from fighting, Jake turned and fired at Sam, once or twice. Iva Wills corroborated this testimony of Sam's, noting that one

Authorities reminded the jailors of Sam's having escaped from their jail on a previous occasion, so that they would give him no opportunity to repeat that performance.[8]

The coroner's jury verdict read, "Jacob Shockey came to death as the result of a gunshot wound at the hand of Samuel Shockey, his brother, aided and abetted by Iva Shockey, wife of Jacob Shockey."[9]

The police also arrested Mrs. Charles Woodring (mother of Catherine) and Paul Crilley as material witnesses to the crime,[10] but both were later released.[11]

During preliminary proceedings, Mrs. Woodring testified that she had heard a scream and a shot shortly after Jacob Shockey walked up the road from her house, where he had gone looking for his wife. She also testified that, after she had heard the shot, she had talked with Samuel Shockey. He was bleeding at the nose and mouth and had bloody hands. She also noticed blood on the shotgun, which Sam explained by saying that he had taken Jake's gun from him.[12]

The trial of Samuel Shockey for the murder of Jacob Shockey opened on April 30. The Commonwealth conducted its case on the theory that the brothers were jealous over Iva Wills. Sam's plea of self-defense relied on Jacob's drinking and his temperament on the day of the murder being considered mitigating factors. Newspapers reported that Iva Wills, who would be tried separately, "was attractively dressed and cheerful as she sat in court watching the tedious process of selecting the jurors. She was the cynosure of all eyes. Her red hair has been bobbed. She wore a neat fitting suit and a close fitting turban.

"Shockey, also of slight build, attentively watched the selection

---

of Jake's shots even pierced Sam's hat. PSI will revisit these issues at a future meeting.—*Ed.*

  [8] "Murderer Says He was Shot at by His Brother," *The Record-Herald, supra,* p. 5, col. 3.

  [9] "Brother and Wife of Victim Held in Mountain Slaying," *supra.*

  [10] *Ibid.*

  [11] "Youthful Widow Held for Death With Companion," *Harrisburg Telegraph,* March 22, 1924, p. 1.

  [12] "Youthful Widow Held for Death," *Harrisburg Telegraph,* March 22, 1924, p. 11.

of jurors. He, too, was well dressed."[13]

Dr. H. C. Bridgers, of Blue Ridge Summit, was the first prosecution witness. He had been called shortly after the body was discovered, and opined that he arrived within an hour after death occurred. He testified that the fatal wound entered the body under the left shoulder blade from behind.[14]

On May 1, the Commonwealth rested. The first defense witness was the coroner, Dr. S. D. Shull. He stated that Jacob Shockey's fatal wounds would not have permitted him to speak after being shot. This refuted the assertion of the police that Sam had told them that when Jake lay dying he told Sam, "You ————, I'll get you."

Then Samuel Shockey took the stand in his own defense. He recounted, "with cold calmness," as the newspaper reported, the facts of the case which only he (and perhaps Iva Wills) could have known. "He told of shooting his brother, feeling his pulse after he had fallen to the ground, covering the body with underbrush and of the flight into the mountains with Iva Wills, the abuse of whom by Jacob was one of the principal factors in the quarrel."[15]

Sam also explained that he and Jake had agreed to meet at Beartown on the day of the shooting.

> "At the home of Clyde Crilley, which he passed en route to Beartown, he met Iva Wills and Catherine Woodring, thirteen years old. Paul Crilly told him, he said, that Jake was hunting for him and was 'going to blow his head off.' Iva informed him, Sam continued, that Jake was drunk and that she was afraid of him. 'I told her,' testified Sam, 'that I would go to see him and see what I could do with him as I always had a good bit of influence with him."[16]

Sam's version of the confrontation at the fork in the road was as follows:—

> "Sam, Iva and Catherine Woodring saw Jake approaching. When he saw them he raised his .22 rifle to his shoulder and demanded:

---

[13] *The Evening News*, April 30, 1924, p. 1.

[14] *The Evening News*, May 1, 1924, p. 17.

[15] "Shockey Takes Stand; Pleads Self Defense," *The Record-Herald*, May 2, 1924, p. 1, col. 7.

[16] *Ibid.*

'Stick 'em up,' Sam said, and then launched into abuse of the girl and himself. As Jake approached menacingly with the gun to his shoulder Sam said he stood with his hands up. Jake struck Iva over the face and then clubbing his gun pushed it into his (Sam's) face.

"'Iva ran behind me or to the side of me,' Sam narrated, 'and I grappled with Jake. We went down three times. The third time we got up Jake broke loose, grabbed his rifle and started away. He had walked only a few steps when he turned and fired twice. One of the shots went past my ear; the other went through my cap.

"'If you pump another shot into that gun, I'll have to get you,' Sam warned.

"Undeterred, Jake shifted the magazine. "'I'll kill you this time; you're afraid to shoot,'" Sam quoted Jake as saying. 'Then he began to turn around with the gun to his shoulder and I shot,' declared Sam with an air of finality. 'He fell and never moved. He said nothing. I went over to him and picked up his hand but could not feel his pulse beating. We then started out the road towards the tent. I met Fannie Woodring and told her that Jake had tried to shoot me and that I had beat him to it.'

"Sam continued that he then noticed that he had lost the fore-piece of his gun. He went back to the scene of the combat and then dragged Jake's body to the side of the road and covered it with underbrush.

"'I was scared,' said Sam, 'for I knew the officers would be after me and wouldn't take my word. The officers had been after me for some time for forgery.'

"After covering the body, Sam again started towards the tent in the mountains. He washed the blood from his face and hands, he said, and then started for Beartown to tell his brothers that he had killed Jake and to await the arrival of officers. When he arrived at Clyde Crilly's house, Mrs. Crilly informed him that Jake's body had been found. This so disconcerted Sam that he turned around and retreated into the mountains."[17]

When twenty-year-old Iva Wills testified, she gained a certain degree of sympathy from her audience. Hers was a—

"story replete with incidents of abuse suffered at the hands of Jake Shockey on the day he was killed," the local newspaper reported. "A girl, far away from home, the man with whom she had cast her lot turning his hand against her—that was the picture Iva, pretty in a wistful way, told in a momentous [*sic*] undertone. She was afraid of Jake, she said. He had demanded that she leave Beartown and

---

[17] *Ibid.,* pp. 1, col. 7, and 5, col. 3.

the only place she had to go was Columbus, Ohio. She went to Samuel, or rather chanced upon him according to her story, and he decided to try to patch up the difficulties that had separated Jake and his flame-haired consort."[18]

Iva endured cross-examination calmly. She testified to the effect that she had had little opportunity in life. She admitted that she had come to Franklin county from Michigan with Jake but was not married to him. They dwelt at Christian Shockey's residence except for one night. Earlier on the day of the shooting, Jake had told her to leave or he would throw her out. He left the house, but returned while she was packing her suitcase. He threw gifts he had given her out the window, and burnt their love letters. After again leaving in his automobile, Jake returned intoxicated, went into the house and retrieved his .22 rifle. Later, when Jake was roaming about the settlement looking for her, Iva was hiding in a closet in Fannie Woodring's house; thence she went to Clyde Crilley's place, where she saw Sam.[19]

Christian Shockey, brother of Jake and Sam, corroborated Iva Wills's allegations of Jake's abusive conduct. He said that Jake was a "dangerous man" when angered and that on the day of his death Jake had acted like a crazy person.[20]

Numerous other defense witnesses described Jacob Shockey as "dangerous," "treacherous," and "mean when drunk." Several of them could testify that Jake had threatened to kill either Iva, Sam, or his brother Chris.[21]

The defense rested on May 2. On May 3, after deliberating for three and three-quarters hours, the jury rendered its verdict of guilty of murder in the second degree. Iva Wills's case was continued to October with slight possibility she would be convicted. Neither she nor Sam made statements following the verdict.[22] The court denied Sam's motion for a new trial.

---

[18] *Ibid.*, p. 5, col. 3.

[19] *Ibid.*

[20] *Ibid.*

[21] "Shockey's Fate Remains with Jury Tonight," *The Record-Herald*, May 3, 1924, p. 6, col. 3.

[22] "Find Shockey Guilty of 2nd Degree Murder," *The Record-Herald*, May 5, 1924, p. 1, col. 7.

In the end, the court sentenced Samuel Shockey to serve nine to eighteen years in Eastern Penitentiary, Philadelphia. The district attorney had requested the maximum allowable sentence, but defense counsel Edmund C. Wingerd made an impassioned plea for leniency in view of all the extenuating circumstances. The other defense counsel, John W. Hoke, asserted that knowledge of Sam's prior criminal record had prejudiced the jury. He speculated that, given the evidence in the case, a man of good reputation would have been acquitted in a few minutes.[23]

In October 1924, authorities released Iva Wills, who had been held as an accessory. Public sentiment was that the girl had been rather more sinned against than guilty of murder.

᠊᠊᠊᠊᠊᠊●᠊᠊᠊᠊᠊᠊

In January 1928, Sam Shockey escaped from prison. Although there are several stories about how he escaped—hiding in a laundry wagon, walking away from a work detail—the official report states that on January 11 Sam escaped by slipping out of a bunk shack used by convicts working on the new penitentiary near Graterford, Pennsylvania.

On February 3, 1928, investigators traced Sam Shockey to the home of Charles Wade, near Cascade, Maryland. There they found his prison garb and gun. Sam himself escaped into the woods near the fire tower on Mount Quirauk, and the officers lost his trail. The following week, various stories would be told of Sam's disappearing into the mountains, the same mountains where he had played as a small boy and where he had hunted and trapped as an adult. If he did not want to be found, he would not be found.[24]

On the morning of February 11, 1928, Sam Shockey told his brother Christian that he wished to surrender but would do so only to Officer Heefner of the Waynesboro Police Department. He asked Chris to meet him at Deer Lick Rock at 1:30 that after-

---

[23] "Samuel Shockey is Given 9 Years," *The Gettysburg Times*, June 9, 1924, p. 1.

[24] "Prison Uniforms and Gun of Shockey Found," *The Record Herald* (Waynesboro, Pa.), February 10, 1928, p. 1, col. 6.

noon to give him a shave and haircut. Chris agreed.

Arriving at the Deer Lick at 1:30, Christian Shockey found Sam's dead body lying upon a rock.[25] He notified the local police, and at 5:00 P.M. Sam's body was taken to E. H. Nickel's funeral home on South Church street, Waynesboro. [26]

At first, the authorities were inclined to believe that Sam's death was a suicide; but his brother Christian would not accept that conclusion, and the coroner concurred that the wounds could not have been self-inflicted. An examination of Samuel Shockey's body disclosed that he had been shot once in the chest, once in the abdomen, and possibly struck in the head with an axe.[27] As an alternative, officers suggested that Sam had fallen while climbing the rocks, his gun accidently discharging in the process; but again Chris objected, and again the coroner's findings supported his position.

Coroner Shull conducted an inquest at the Nickel Funeral Home, and his jury ruled that Sam met his death by hands of an unknown person or persons.[28]

Several thousand persons visited Nickel's to view Sam Shockey's corpse, but only a small group of family and friends braved cold, wet weather to attend graveside services in the Calvary Episcopal graveyard, Beartown.[29]

Forest Ranger Harry Thomas headed a party to search for Sam Shockey's camp in the mountains. Their efforts prevailed when they found a well-camouflaged, well-stocked canvas and oilcloth shack. Most of the property inside had been stolen from nearby

---

[25] "Shockey Found with Top of Head Blown Off," *The Record Herald*, February 11, 1928, p. 1.

[26] A photograph made at the scene corroborates the tradition that Samuel Shockey was found with his trousers lowered to his ankles, and that his brother Chris raised them so that Sam would be covered when photographed. A dusting of snow had fallen on the corpse, but the photograph shows that the trousers alone were free of snow. This fact has given rise to the belief that Sam was killed by someone who was enraged by finding him in a compromising situation.—*Ed.*

[27] The coroner certified that Samuel Shockey died as the result of "Gunshot wounds of chest & abdomen—also fractured skull—caused by an unknown hand" (Commonwealth of Pennsylvania Certificate of Death #21247).

[28] "Jury Decides Unknown Persons Killed Shockey," *The Record Herald*, February 14, 1928, p. 1.

[29] "Body of Sam Shockey Buried at Beartown," *The Record Herald*, *supra*, p. 1, col. 8.

hunting camps, and was afterwards returned to its various own-
ers. Interestingly, this tent was situated only about two hundred
yards from the old cabin of Henry Heist who was hanged for the
murder of Emanuel Monn thirty-five years beforehand.[30]

Several persons were arrested for aiding Sam Shockey during
his flight, but no one has ever been charged with his murder,
though suspicion has fallen on various local residents through
the years. After the lapse of almost ninety years, it is unlikely
that the case will ever be solved.

[*Editor's Note: The Waynesboro newspaper closed its coverage
of the manhunt for escapee Sam Shockey with an editorial which
exudes so much enlightenment that it is also a fitting means of closing this retrospective about the murders of the Shockey brothers. Its
message is as relevant today as it was almost a century ago:*]

"Call it retribution or what you like, and it makes no difference in
the facts. Samuel Shockey, the fugitive, has been slain. Yesterday
his funeral was held. Tribute, honest, sincere tribute, was paid his
memory by his friends of the Beartown section. To them his 'faults
were written upon the sands'—they chose to remember him simply as Sam Shockey, a likeable chap of the mountains and one they
loved for his goodness. They did not choose to remember 'Sam' as a
'bad boy.' They chose to remember 'Sam' as a 'good boy.'

"He had his good points. He made his mistakes, as Rev. Pfaffko
pointed out in his funeral service—but he was one of God's children
and who is there to judge. This minister spoke of the powerful les-
son taught by the case so recently brought to tragic light. He said
that no one could know how good were the thoughts in the heart
of the man, nor how great an influence matters of environment had
upon him.

One can moralize now that Shockey is gone. Shockey was not
of the calibre of the young slayers who victimize childhood, nor of
the New Jersey variety of slayer. He was a simple mountain boy,
influenced by the traditions of the mountains. This is a reminder
of the point made by the minister at the funeral. 'How responsible
are all of us?' he asked. 'How responsible are we for the mistakes
of our brother?'"[31]

---

[30] Hut Believed Occupied by Shockey Found," *The Record Herald*, *supra*, p. 1,
col. 7.

[31] "Shockey's Passing," *The Record Herald*, February 15, 1928, p. 4, col. 1.

III.
Peabody Bank Robbery Ring.

TODD ANDREW DORSETT.

March 12, 2013.

Twenty-seven persons attended the third meeting of the Potomac Street Irregulars, held at the Parlor House.

I N 1939, an intelligent, personable, bespectacled radio technician named Gerard Peabody opened a radio store on Center square, Waynesboro, Pennsylvania. He preferred to be called "Jerry." The townspeople liked him. He offered the town's school children an interesting Saturday diversion: their own radio show. Several months later, Waynesboro chief burgess J. W. Croft noted that Jerry had told him he was going to put Waynesboro on the map. He did; but the town would have gladly forgone the publicity, for Jerry Peabody was a bank robber.[1]

Gerard Rushton Peabody was born at Seattle, King county, Washington, on February 26, 1900. He was the fifth of eight sons of Charles Enoch Peabody (1857–1926) and his wife, *nee* Lilly Harriet Macauley (1870–1944). C. E. Peabody had been a New York stockbroker who followed his familial instincts into shipping. He settled in the State of Washington, where he married the daughter of a prosperous Canadian businessman. C. E. Peabody subsequently made a large fortune as president of the Alaska Steamship and Puget Sound Navigation companies. Eventually his family would monopolize the ferry business on Puget Sound, operating under the famous Black Ball flag Peabody's ancestors had flown on their transatlantic ships.

Several of the eight Peabody sons were spirited lads. While still a minor, Jerry's brother Penfield eloped with a dairymaid, with his irate father in hot pursuit. The youngest brother, Duane,

---

[1] *The Record Herald* (Waynesboro, Pa.), October 5, 1985, p. 5, cols. 1-6.

was a state policeman for a while, but Jerry's other siblings tended to business. C. E. Peabody's second son, Captain Alexander Marshall Peabody, succeeded his father at the helm. By his teen years, however, Jerry himself was considered "bad."[2] After matriculating at the elite Tome School in Cecil county, Maryland, he ran away.[3] Whether at his parents' instigation or of his own volition, Jerry spent the period between September 1916 and March 1917 at sea, headquartered at Calleo, Peru.

In November 1917, Gerard Peabody moved to Sydney, Australia. Supposedly, during his stay in Australia he joined the Victoria Mounted Police and served as a flight lieutenant in the British Army during the First World War.[4]

Also during his Australian sojourn, Peabody married Miss Rose Ella Craggs, who was born in England in 1896. In January 1920 Jerry returned to the United States, bringing Rose Ella with him. She died at Seattle in 1971.

Upon returning to Washington, Gerard Peabody made an unsuccessful attempt to work in the family business. After repeated quarrels with his "miserly" father, Jerry left Seattle and claimed to have commenced working as a police officer at Portland, Oregon.[5]

Gerard and Rose Ella Peabody had three children. Gerardine Florence Peabody was born in 1921 at Portland, Oregon. Gerard Charles Peabody was born in New York in 1923. And Bernice Peabody was born in 1925, when Jerry was working as a mechanic at Newark, New Jersey. Around that time, Jerry's recorded legal difficulties began. A conviction for receiving a stolen car[6] earned him eighteen months in the New Jersey State Reformatory at Rahway.

Following his release from prison, Gerard Peabody moved his operations to Baltimore, Maryland. In that city, he robbed several grocery stores. On June 4, 1930, this spree resulted in a

---

[2] *See* "Bank Robber Once Wealthy," *The Daily Mail* (Hagerstown, Md.), January 31, 1940, p. 3, col. 1.

[3] *The Record Herald, supra.*

[4] *Ibid. See also The Record Herald*, January 30, 1940, p. 1, col. 6.

[5] *Ibid.*

[6] *Ibid.*

conviction for robbery with a dangerous weapon. He received a sentence of fifteen years imprisonment. He served eight years of that sentence.[7]

While incarcerated in Maryland, Peabody became tubercular. Because the prison had no hospital facilities for the treatment of tuberculosis, Jerry was paroled to the State Sanatorium near Sabillasville, in the mountains of Frederick county.[8] During his stay in the sanatorium, Gerard Peabody cultivated a relationship with a fellow patient, Miss Ruth Hall, formerly of Cumberland, Maryland. He filed a bill of complaint in Frederick County Court for absolute divorce from Rose Ella Peabody.[9] The marriage was dissolved, and on December 22, 1939, Jerry married Miss Hall.

Upon release from the sanatorium, May 24, 1938, Gerard Peabody erected and occupied a one-room combination dwelling house and repair shop on the south side of the new Military road at Cullen, between Sabillasville and Highfield. On the pretense of having a large Waynesboro clientele, he soon opened a radio store in the old Grange hall, northeast corner of Center square, Waynesboro.[10] This store was his only connexion to the Antietam country; none of his heists actually occurred here.

The relationship of Gerard Peabody with the people of Waynesboro presaged some episodes of *The Andy Griffith Show.* Jerry descended on Waynesboro with charm and talent, opening a legitimate radio store. The workbench of "Jerry's" radio repair, equipment, and electrical appliance shop was located in the store's front window, within plain view of the town's two largest financial institutions.[11] He ingratiated himself with the townsfolk, and sponsored a weekly Saturday children's radio show, "The Original Waynesboro Kiddie Klub," which he broadcast from the back room of his store and aired on a Western Maryland station. "Uncle Jerry" was indeed making good on his promise to put Waynesboro on the map.[12]

---

[7] *Ibid.* See also *The Record Herald,* January 30, 1940, p. 1, col. 6.

[8] *The Record Herald,* January 30, 1940, p. 1, col. 6.

[9] "Court News," *The Frederick Post* (Frederick, Md.), June 22, 1939, p. 2, col. 5.

[10] *See* "Mountain Retreat," *The Record Herald,* February 5, 1940, p. 1, cols. 4-5.

[11] *The Record Herald,* January 30, 1940, p. 1, col. 6.

[12] *The Record Herald,* October 5, 1985, *supra.*

Peabody also became involved in Waynesboro civic activities. One ironic twist to the story is that he operated the public address system in the auditorium of Waynesboro Senior High School during the Waynesboro Exchange Club's staging of the play "Lyric Time," a story about a "city slicker" who descends upon a country town to commit a big heist.[13]

During Gerard Peabody's few months in Waynesboro, he was involved in only one unseemly incident of which there is any record. He and a "Lyric Time" performer almost came to blows outside the basement lounge of the Hotel Anthony Wayne over Peabody's attentions to the other man's sweetheart following the play's final performance.[14]

Meanwhile, someone was robbing banks across rural Maryland, with employees and customers being locked in the banks' vaults at gunpoint.[15] The first of these occurred on October 22, 1939, at White Hall, Baltimore county. Six days later, the same robbers returned to White Hall to get, they said, the ten thousand dollars they had left behind the first time.

On December 20, 1939, the bandits robbed a bank at Clear Spring, in the western part of Washington county. And on January 16, 1940, at 9:25 A.M., they hit the Walkersville Bank, Frederick county.

These four robberies netted the perpetrators a total of more than fifteen thousand dollars, of which sixty-six hundred was taken during the final crime. Much of this was in coin. Several thousand dollars was recovered during the police investigation of the robberies.[16]

On or about January 29, 1940, Federal Bureau of Investigation agents and Maryland state police arrested four men in connexion with these robberies:

1. SIDNEY JAMES OWEN THOMPSON had been refused parole from his last prison sentence, so served his entire term. His au-

---

[13] "When We Harbored a Bank Robber," *The Record Herald*, February 3, 1979, p. 4, col. 1.

[14] *Ibid.*

[15] "Witnesses Identify 4 Accused as Robbers," *The Record Herald*, March 5, 1940, p. 1., col. 3.

[16] *The Record Herald*, January 30, 1940, p. 1, col. 6.

tomobile was used as the "get-away" car. Police found it abandoned, and it contained numerous clues to the participants in
the robberies. Thompson turned state's evidence, pled guilty to
all four robberies, and implicated Gerard Peabody in his crimes.

    2. DALLAS HILARY WHIPP, like Peabody, had been paroled
to the Sanatorium while serving six years for burglary. He pled
guilty to the Walkersville bank robbery. The discovery of horn-
rimmed spectacles belonging to him in the abandoned "get-
away" car was a major breakthrough in the investigation.

    3. WILLIAM WESLEY DUNNOCK, who, like Thompson, had been
refused parole from his last prison sentence, pled guilty to the
Walkersville bank robbery.

    4. GERARD RUSHTON PEABODY, on parole from a fifteen-year
sentence for armed robbery, was accused as the ringleader, and
stood trial in federal court.[17]

Despite a great deal of incriminating evidence, Gerard Peabody
pled not guilty to the bank robbery charges.[18] His co-defendants
readily provided evidence against him. The police report contained this statement:

"Peabody, who presents the appearance of a middle-aged businessman, was referred to by his companions as the 'man with the front', and
is reputed to have told these associates that his purpose for operating
the business was a 'blind', and he actually spent little or no time han-
dling the details of his business.

"He is likewise alleged to have made the statement during his previous incarceration, on his release that he was going to make some money
to reimburse him for the time spent in the penitentiary, and was going
to make it fast through bank robberies.

"A search of his residence, the officers among other things located articles dealing with Alcatraz, also a .30-.30 Marlin lever action rifle, which
was purchased after the robbery of the White Hall bank on the first occasion, and which he explained to associates, was to be used to prevent
pursuit in future 'jobs'."[19]

---

[17] *See The Gettysburg Times* (Gettysburg, Pa.), March 7, 1940, p. 1, col. 3; *The
Record Herald,* January 30, 1940, p. 1, col. 6.

[18] *The Record Herald,* October 5, 1985, *supra.*

[19] "Highfield Resident Held," *The Record Herald,* January 30, 1940, p. 8, col. 5.

On February 6, 1940, a federal grand jury in Baltimore indicted Gerard Peabody for all four Maryland bank robberies.[20] Jerry reiterated his plea of not guilty, and his trial commenced on March 4, 1940. On the following day, the court recessed for one day after the prosecution presented a witness who identified Peabody as the ringleader who ordered the other robbers to scoop up the bank money and force employees into the vault.[21] Subsequently, the cashier at First National Bank of Blue Ridge Summit, Edgar McClain, testified that Peabody had made large deposits between October 28, 1939, and January 16, 1940, the time period during which the bank robberies occurred. Edward F. Croney, an employee in Peabody's Waynesboro shop, testified that Peabody

was not in the store until after noon on the day the Walkersville bank was robbed some forty miles away. The United States rested its case on March 8.[22]

Whipp testified for the prosecution that Peabody had told him the Walkersville robbery would be Peabody's last; that he had recently married, and that he wanted to settle down at his radio repair shop.[23] Whether that was true will forever remain a mystery.

During the defense case, the well-respected superintendent of the Maryland State Sanatorium, Dr. Victor Cullen, testified that Gerard Peabody was "an honest and respectable citizen" of the mountain community. He also noted that several days before Christmas 1939 Jerry had left ten dollars at his residence, with directions that Cullen use the money for a children's fund at the sanatorium. The youthful second Mrs. Gerard Peabody testified that Jerry had been with her when the Clear Spring bank had

---

[20] "Four Indicted in Holdups," *The Record Herald*, February 7, 1940, p. 1, col. 2; p. 8, col. 4.

[21] "Trial of Four Bank Robbers Delayed a Day," *Evening Times* (Cumberland, Md.), March 5, 1940, p. 2, col. 7.

[22] "Cumberland Girl Wife of Accused Bandit," *Cumberland Evening Times* (Cumberland, Md.), March 5, 1940, p. 2, col. 7.

[23] "Trial of Bank Robbers," *The Record Herald*, March 7, 1940, p. 7, col. 6.

been robbed.[24] But most importantly, the Waynesboro chief of police, Floyd Maurer, testified that he had seen Peabody in his Center square store between 10:00 and 10:45 A.M.

Chief Maurer, aged thirty-three years, joined the Waynesboro police force ten years before the Peabody trial, shortly after leaving the Pennsylvania State Police. Six years after borough council elected him to the local force, he was named chief. Cross-examination failed to alter Chief Maurer's testimony that he had seen Peabody at his Waynesboro store the morning of the Walkersville robbery. This led defense counsel Felkin to ask the jury, "Which will you believe, the chief of police, or frightened bank clerks who thought they saw this mild-looking defendant at the scene of the crime?"[25]

A number of Blue Ridge Summit residents were summoned as witnesses, including the bookkeeper of the First National Bank of Blue Ridge Summit.[26]

The jury convicted Gerard Peabody. On March 8, 1940, Judge William C. Coleman sentenced him to serve twenty-two years in prison on each of the four counts and pay a fine of five thousand dollars. The court ordered that Peabody's sentences should run concurrently, so that the net effect of the sentences was twenty-two years in prison.[27] After the court denied all post-trial motions on Peabody's behalf, Jerry was transferred to the federal penitentiary at Atlanta, Georgia. The Peabody family made full restitution in Gerard's behalf.

One month later, the Waynesboro borough council asked Chief Maurer for his resignation. The published reason for this action was that there was a discrepancy in the subpœna requiring his presence at the Peabody trial. The chief resigned his position effective April 8, 1940.[28] During Borough Council's investigation, documents surfaced indicating that Maurer, whom the defense

---

[24] *Ibid.* Still being treated for tuberculosis, Mrs. Peabody on one occasion appeared in court wearing a black veil, and confirmed that she had met Peabody while both were patients at the sanatorium. *The Record Herald*, March 7, 1940.

[25] "Peabody Given 22 Years," *The Record Herald*, March 9, 1940, p. 6, col. 3.

[26] "Blue Ridge Summit," *The Record Herald*, March 7, 1940, p. 9, col. 2.

[27] "Peabody Given 22 Years," *The Record Herald*, March 9, 1940, p. 1, col. 4.

[28] "Police Chief Resigns," *The Frederick Post*, April 10, 1940, p. 9, col. 8; "When We Harbored a Bank Robber," *supra.*

summoned to testify, received the subpœna upon his arrival in Baltimore for the trial. Maurer, on the other hand, told the council that a United States Marshal had served him at Waynesboro police headquarters.[29] The general opinion is that the chief volunteered to help Jerry Peabody in his trial.[30]

Despite Gerard Peabody's receiving only one misconduct report at Atlanta, federal prison officials described him as "a shrewd, intelligent, prison-wise individual with a deep-seated antipathy toward institutional control." They used this evaluation to recommend Jerry's transfer from Atlanta to the federal prison on Alcatraz Island in San Francisco Bay, reasoning that he "associated himself with the more violent, dangerous and troublemaking type prisoner and has required extremely close supervision on this account."

One writer has noted, however, that it was difficult to fill the cells at Alcatraz at that time, and that the system probably transferred Peabody in order to fill a bed as much as for the stated reasons. In addition, Jerry's appeals to federal court regarding the terms of his sentence and subsequent treatment while at Atlanta might have influenced prison officials in recommending the transfer. At all events, in July 1945, even though he was not among "the worst of the worst," Gerard Peabody was removed to Alcatraz.

On Alcatraz, Jerry Peabody was a model prisoner. In the three years he spent on "the rock," Jerry received no misconduct reports, and prison officials noted that he was "friendly and cheerful." He would later relate that he much preferred the routine at Alcatraz to sleeping in a cell with multiple inmates in Atlanta or the ever-changing rules of McNeil Island, where he would later reside.

In November 1948, Gerard Peabody was again transferred between federal prisons. This time, he settled in on McNeil Island, near Tacoma in his native State. After Maryland agreed to lift a detainer against Peabody for a parole violation, his family could

---

[29] "Investigation is Continued," *The Record Herald*, March 22, 1940, p. 1, col. 8.

[30] After leaving Waynesboro, Floyd L. Maurer became a security guard. On December 22, 1956, he died suddenly from a heart attack at his home in Camp Hill, Pa., and lies buried with his wife in Evergreen Cemetery, Gettysburg, Pa.

visit him. His daughters visited him fairly regularly.[31]

In November 1953, the federal prison system conditionally released Gerard R. Peabody. The following year found him residing in Seattle, where he became a bartender.

On June 6, 1954, in the ballroom of the Fort Cumberland Hotel, Cumberland, Maryland, Mrs. Mary Ann Brown, *nee* Clark, of Pittsburgh and Cumberland, became the third wife of Gerard Rushton Peabody. Gerard C. Peabody acted as his father's best man, and the younger's wife served as a bridesmaid. The newspaper announcement of the marriage stated that Jerry was then associated with the Puget Sound Navigation Company. The bridal couple planned to settle in Seattle.[32]

On November 19, 1956, someone robbed the West Seattle branch of the People's National Bank of Washington. That heist netted the robbers more than forty-two thousand dollars, of which the authorities recovered a considerable amount. On November 20, the police arrested four persons for the West Seattle robbery: Gerard Peabody for bank robbery; Raymond William Joseph Clermont for bank robbery; and Jane Hardesty and Mary McGraw as material witnesses.[33]

Once again, Gerard R. Peabody stood trial for bank robbery. During an overnight court recess, he overdosed on drugs he had accumulated and hidden. He fell unconscious and revived only after drastic emergency treatment.

On April 23, 1957, a jury convicted Gerard Peabody on seven counts, and the court sentenced him to serve thirty years in prison. Despite his age and nonviolent personality, the system returned him to Alcatraz. There he was either cooperative or detached.

> "At his annual review meetings, Peabody either asked to be excused or remained 'absolutely mute throughout the interview.' He had six brothers, two ex-wives, two daughters, and a son but did

---

[31] David Ward with Gene Kassebaum, *Alcatraz: The Gangster Years* (Berkeley and Los Angeles, Calif.: University of California Press, 2009), pp. 434*ff.*

[32] *The Cumberland News* (Cumberland, Md.), June 11, 1954, p. 6.

[33] "14,000 of Bank Loot Recovered," *Walla Walla Union-Bulletin* (Walla Walla, Wash.), December 14, 1956, p. 1, col. 6; Ward, *supra.*

not correspond with or receive visits from any of them. He continued to avoid misconduct reports, received good work reports, and was described as 'popular' with other prisoners. His health problems and 'nervousness' increased, however."[34]

In anticipation of the closing of Alcatraz in March 1963, Gerard Peabody was transferred to McNeil Island in December 1962. In July 1965, however, after being reported as assisting other prisoners "in plotting and planning escapes," prison officials recommended that he be transferred to a high-security facility. Consequently, in September of that year, prison officials saw fit to return a sixty-five-year-old offender to Atlanta.

In October 1966, Jerry was transferred back to McNeil Island, where he did well, but had "resigned himself to dying in prison." When he became eligible for parole, he refused to apply because he was unwilling to admit guilt.

In June 1972, Gerard Peabody did apply for parole, stating, "I am 74 years of age and have only a few years to live. . . . I am old, infirmed [*sic*], ill and am unable to be a threat to anyone . . . at my age there is little left in life except a few years of quiet living with my children and grandchildren." In February 1974, an aged Gerard Peabody was paroled from McNeil Island.[35]

Be that as it may . . .

On April 18, 1974, armed robbers stole eleven hundred twenty-two dollars from the Pacific National Bank in Seattle. In June of the same year, someone stole seventeen thousand five hundred nine dollars from the Ballard Bank of Washington. The same year, armed robbers netted thirty-two thousand dollars from the Seattle First National Bank branch in Duvall, Washington.

At the time of the foregoing crimes, Gerard Peabody had been sentenced to serve a total of one hundred eleven years for fifteen felony convictions.

---

[34] Ward at 435.
[35] Ward, *supra*.

Round up the usual suspects, and work your snitches.

Gerard Peabody again found himself in custody, accused as the leader of a bank robbery ring. With him were arrested the following three accomplices:

1. J. H. "BLACKIE" AUDETT, aged seventy-two years, career bank robber and author of the book *Rap Sheet*, in which he claimed friendship with Al Capone, "Machine Gun" Kelly, and other Prohibition-era gangsters;

2. ARMANDO JOHN VARGAS, aged twenty-seven years;

3. DENNIS PATRICK NOLAN, aged twenty-two years.[36]

Convicted of the bank robberies in Washington, Peabody returned to McNeil Island, and would never again be free. In April 1978, at the age of seventy-eight years, he was transferred to the Federal Medical Center at Springfield, Missouri, for treatment of cataracts in both eyes and cancer. By this time he was a "bed-to-wheelchair invalid" and was considered for parole.

No member of the Peabody family would accept responsibility for Jerry. One of his daughters told authorities that one of her own daughters had vowed she would leave home if he were allowed to live there. With no other option, the federal authorities paroled Gerard Peabody to a nursing home. On August 6, 1980, he was flown to a nursing facility in Seattle, and on December 23, 1980, heart disease and cancer ended the arduous life of Gerard Rushton Peabody.[37]

"Jerry" Peabody inherited hundreds of thousands of dollars from his parents' estates[38]—equal to millions of dollars today. Clearly he had no need to rob banks for money. Then why did

---

[36] "Aged Bank Robber Adds Chapter to Crime Saga," *Pasadena Star-News* (Pasadena, Calif.), June 16, 1974, p. A-9, col. 1.

[37] In 1985 the Waynesboro newspaper ran several articles about Gerard Peabody's sojourn in this region. The writers made the easy mistake of researching him under the name "Gerald Peabody," and relied on faulty information about his life after being convicted of the Maryland bank robberies. He did not die in a Maryland prison, and was indeed the elderly bank robber in Washington State in 1974, contrary to "End of the Peabody Story," *The Record Herald,* October 12, 1985, p. 4, col. 1.

[38] "Bank Robber Once Wealthy," *supra.*

he do it? Perhaps, like Nathan Leopold and Richard Loeb, also sons of wealthy families of the same era, he committed crimes for the thrill.

At the time of his arrest in Maryland, parole records included the opinion that Gerard Peabody was "consistently anti-social."[39] Obviously he was at least mildly sociopathic; that is, his behavior disregarded the consequences to others. Experts tell us that sociopaths make great politicians, among other powerful occupations.

Or perhaps Jerry's problem lay in his genes. His paternal grandfather, Enoch Wood Peabody, a wealthy sea captain, was charged in 1866 with cruelty for beating and otherwise abusing his crew and passengers aboard the *Neptune*. The complainant in the case against Captain Peabody, one Amos Richards, had been so badly beaten that he lost the use of his arms.[40] Gerard Peabody, bank robber, seems harmless in comparison with his sea captain grandfather.

Consider, also, Gerard's brother Captain Alexander M. Peabody, who succeeded their father as president of the family business: he was willing to bring the entire city of Seattle to its knees and cripple transportation on Puget Sound in order to squeeze more money out of the city and county governments while forcing them to purchase his Black Ball ferry lines. In contrast, often the money Jerry stole from banks was recovered or restitution was quickly paid.

Whose actions are worse? Why is some malevolent behaviour illegal and some not?

However one answers those poignant questions, it is a fact that pivotal events in this fascinating story occurred right here in the Antietam country.

---

[39] *Ibid.*

[40] "Cruelty on the High Seas," *The New York Times* (New York, N. Y.), January 12, 1866; "News of the Day," *The New York Times,* January 12, 1866.

IV.
The Murder of Miss Betty Jane Kennedy—Part I.

FRANK BOCK.

April 9, 2013.

The fourth meeting of the Potomac Street Irregulars was held at the Parlor House, with at least seventy persons in attendance. This first presentation by PSI Bock set a precedent for attracting capacity audiences with his thorough research, confident presentation, and wry wit. The slaying of Miss Betty Jane Kennedy remains one of the most intriguing crimes in local history. Because of its complexity, PSI Bock has agreed to revisit the case each April with the hope that the Irregulars can sort through the voluminous information about the case, and solve its mystery.

O N Monday, April 1, 1946, Miss Betty Jane Kennedy, aged eighteen and one-half years, left her home at 498 Mitchell Avenue, Hagerstown, Maryland, vowing never to return. She and the older sister with whom she dwelt, Mrs. Pauline Gonder, had argued over Betty Jane's lifestyle. Pauline cautioned Betty to be more careful; but Betty ignored that warning, and left with a small suitcase containing some of her meagre possessions.

The following day, Betty Kennedy visited the Hagerstown Police Department seeking help from officers in finding employment.

On Wednesday, April 3, Betty Kennedy had dinner with a man in uniform at a restaurant on South Potomac street, Hagerstown. Witnesses identified the man as Earl McFarland, a murderer-rapist who had recently escaped from death row in the District of Columbia. This identification ultimately proved false when the police determined that McFarland had been nowhere near Hagerstown at that time.[1]

---

[1] There were several sightings of Earl McFarland in Western Maryland and Franklin county, Pa., during his flight from death row. When shown recent photographs of Private McFarland, most of the witnesses were absolutely certain that the man they saw was he. The authorities based their elimination of McFar-

Betty Jane Kennedy was reportedly last seen alive later that evening, again with a man in uniform, at the Square Deal Inn on the Leitersburg pike, near Leitersburg, Maryland. Betty and the uniformed man allegedly left the Square Deal after 11:30 P.M. Lulu Knodle, of Hagerstown, later recanted her story that she had seen Miss Kennedy there with a tall, handsome man with shiny dark hair who wore a battle jacket bedecked with ribbons, and who playfully pretended to strangle Betty Jane with a shoe-string.[2]

On Thursday, April 4, around 6:15 A.M., a passing school bus driver saw what he thought was a mannequin lying against a log a short distance off the north side of Buchanan Trail (now Old Route 16) on the South Mountain, one-half mile east of Rouzer-ville, Pennsylvania.

About 8:30 that same morning, while walking along Old Route 16 near his home, eighteen-year-old J. Martin Benchoff noticed a woman's blue-green cloth coat hanging on a sapling in the woods opposite the entrance to his father's property. Upon further in-vestigation, he saw the unclothed body of a young woman lying against a log a short distance west of where the coat dangled from the small tree.[3] Benchoff telephoned the Waynesboro po-lice, who dispatched an officer to the mountain. Pennsylvania State Police assigned Detective Sergeant Carl E. Hartman of

---

land as a suspect in the Kennedy murder on McFarland's own statement. After being captured at Knoxville, Tenn., McFarland told police that he had crossed the Potomac river to Alexandria, Va., shortly after his escape and hitchhiked to his native Knoxville *via* Richmond, Va. PSI has not eliminated McFarland as a sus-pect in the Kennedy case, because there was adequate time for him to have been in Maryland and Pennsylvania during his flight; because Miss Kennedy's stran-gulation matches his *modus operandi*, and because several witnesses identified him as Miss Kennedy's companion. At the same time, PSI considers it unlikely that Private McFarland, during his flight, would have interacted socially and publicly as witnessed described. PSI therefore place little emphasis upon him as a suspect in the Kennedy murder.—*Ed.*

[2] "Denies Knowing About Murder," *The Daily Mail* (Hagerstown, Md.), Janu-ary 26, 1948, p. 1.

[3] The coat bore a Leiter Brothers label. "Identify Body of Young Girl as that of Hagerstown Resident," *The Daily Mail* (Hagerstown, Md.), April 5, 1946, p. 1; "Strangled Woman is Identified," *The Record Herald* (Waynesboro, Pa.), April 5, 1946, p. 1.

its Criminal Division at Harrisburg to the case, and he became Pennsylvania's lead investigator in the case.

Investigators found the woman's almost nude, garrotted body lying face down on a bed of leaves on a cinder-covered, wooded slope between Buchanan Trail and the Sunshine Trail (now Buchanan Trail East). Her head pointed toward the west, and her face was slightly inclined toward the public road. Her arms were folded under her body, and her legs were crossed. Her only clothing was a pink slip rolled up tightly around her torso. A "locust log lodged against two small walnut trees" had prevented her body from descending the embankment to Red run, flowing through the ravine far below. Her coat dangled from the branch of a small tree approximately eight feet east of her body.[4]

Dirt under the woman's fingernails and toenails suggested that she had crawled at least three feet before expiring.[5] She therefore had been alive at that site in Washington township, Franklin county, Pennsylvania.

That afternoon, on her property about one mile east of where the woman's body was found, Mrs. Luther Mummert found an inexpensive brown pocketbook. The purse contained a pair of women's gloves, lipstick, eleven cents in change, and a souvenir pencil-lighter bearing the insignia of the Hagerstown "UAW-CIO."[6]

The autopsy which Franklin County Coroner S. D. Shull and his assistant Dr. J. C. Corbett performed on the woman's corpse at the Grove Funeral Home, Waynesboro, in the evening of April 4 revealed the cause of death as strangulation with a light rope or wire and a broken neck.[7] Dr. Shull noted that it was possible that the woman had been hanged elsewhere and her body moved

---

[4] "Hagerstown Taxi Driver Questioned," *The Record Herald* (Waynesboro, Pa.), April 8, p. 6, col. 4.

[5] "Blood-Stained Trousers Clue," *The Daily Mail* (Hagerstown, Md.), April 8, 1946, p. 2. *See also* "Strangled Woman is Identified," *supra.*

[6] "Betty Jane Kennedy is Found Dead," *The Record Herald*, April 5, 1946, p. 8, col. 1. *See Also* "Suspect Taken into Custody; Rope is Found," *The Morning Herald* (Hagerstown, Md.), April 8, 1946, p. 1.

[7] Allegedly the autopsy also disclosed that Betty Jane was pregnant when she died. Police thought that this might have been the killer's motive. The newspaper reported "a severe bruise to the lower abdomen." Scratches to her abdomen and inner thighs were believed to have been caused by her slayer. *Ibid.*

to the site where Benchoff found it.[8] The scratches and claw marks on the body also gave rise to various theories of what the ill-fated woman had experienced during her final struggle.[9]

Shortly before noon on Friday, April 5, 1946, the sheriff of Washington county, Maryland, John B. Huyett, brought Mrs. John E. Kennedy and her eldest daughter, Mrs. Pauline Gonder, to the Grove Funeral Home. At noon, Mrs. Gonder identified the body as that of her sister Betty Jane Kennedy. The murdered girl's tall, greying mother sobbed continuously as Mrs. Gonder recounted how she had admonished Betty Jane for "running around" and being "with a different fellow every night."[10]

On Saturday, April 6, the body of Betty Jane Kennedy was removed to the Coffman Funeral Home, Hagerstown. Her funeral and burial in Rose Hill Cemetery, Hagerstown, occurred on the afternoon of April 8.[11]

Betty Jane Kennedy was born September 16, 1927, at Hagerstown, the last-born daughter of John E. and Sadie (Butler) Kennedy. At age six, Betty Jane ran into the side of an automobile driving along West Washington street, Hagerstown. She was hospitalized with head cuts and a possible skull fracture. The injuries she sustained during this accident eventually necessitated a skin graft from her thigh to the region above her left eye, leaving an inch-long scar affecting her eyelid.[12] Nevertheless, she was considered pretty as a young woman. She stood approximately five feet seven inches tall, had dark brown hair and brown eyes, and was of "medium slender build."[13] She was known as a "party girl," and her hobby seemed to be men, especially older men. She had quit school at age sixteen, and during the week prior to her

---

[8] "Blood-Stained Trousers Clue," *supra.*

[9] "Shoe Had No Connection," *The Record Herald* (Waynesboro, Pa.), April 11, 1946, p. 12, col. 4.

[10] *Ibid.*

[11] "Blood-Stained Trousers Clue," *supra.*

[12] Grove Funeral Home records, courtesy of Mr. James Fritzinger; "Child Badly Hurt by Car," *The Daily Mail* (Hagerstown, Md.), December 1, 1933, p. 1, col. 8. *See also The Daily Mail* (Hagerstown, Md.), January 31, 1940, p. 6, col. 2, *and* "Strangled Woman is Identified," *supra.*

[13] "Strangled Woman is Identified," *supra.*

death had been working part-time as a waitress at Airport Inn, near the Hagerstown airport.[14]

Law enforcement agencies from several jurisdictions joined in the Kennedy murder investigation. These agencies included the office of Franklin County (Pa.) District Attorney LeRoy S. Maxwell; Detective Sergeant Carl E. Hartman and Officer Oscar Tingley, Pennsylvania State Police criminal bureau at Harrisburg; Chief William H. Peters, Detective Wayne Sellman, and Patrolmen L. C. Karn and Donald Smith, Hagerstown Police Department; Sheriff John B. Huyett, Deputy Bruce Spickler, and County Investigator Thomas Staub, Washington County (Md.) Sheriff's Department; Sergeant James J. Cassidy, Maryland State Police; Major Harvey Callahan, District of Columbia Metropolitan Police; two agents from the Hagerstown office of the Federal Bureau of Investigation; Waynesboro Police Department; Franklin County Sheriff's Department.[15]

During the course of their investigation, these agencies questioned approximately one thousand persons about the Kennedy case. They interviewed three hundred of these more than once. They quickly received over one hundred tips from a public eager to help solve the case. The authorities' primary focus was Earl McFarland, then the nation's most wanted fugitive, but both District Attorney Maxwell and District of Columbia Metropolitan Police soon eliminated him as a suspect after authorities determined he was elsewhere at the time of the Kennedy murder.[16]

Other suspects included a taxicab driver with whom Betty Kennedy was frequently seen, and whom authorities detained without charge; the cab driver's disgruntled wife; the young man who found the body, whom investigators questioned on three oc-

---

[14] "Strangled Woman is Identified," *supra.*

[15] "Blood-Stained Trousers Clue," *supra.*

[16] Private McFarland was recaptured on April 11, 1946, at Knoxville, Tenn. The District of Columbia later executed McFarland, a veteran of Guadalcanal, for the October 5, 1944, rape and garrotting-murder of an eighteen-year-old government clerk, Dorothy Berrum. His alleged *modus operandi*, his status as the nation's most wanted fugitive at the time of the Kennedy murder, and the fact that Betty Kennedy had been seen with a man in uniform probably enlivened the public's imagination about a possible liaison between Private McFarland and the Kennedy girl.

casions; any one of seventeen men with whom Betty was seen after leaving home; a soldier from Security, Maryland, near Hagerstown, who was absent without leave from Walter Reed Army Hospital at the time the murder occurred; a "decorated soldier" with whom Betty was allegedly seen at the Square Deal Inn; a Merchant Marine; William Edgar "Scrappy" Snider, an ex-convict who resided very close to the site where Betty Kennedy's body was found; an ex-convict friend of Snider's, Lawrence Speece, of Ohio; an unidentified companion of Speece's from Virginia; and a former resident of Hagerstown then living at Cumberland, Maryland, who turned himself in when told the police were looking for him.

Authorities had thirty suspects they seriously considered. Several of these were taken into custody but later released. Had they taken the killer into custody and released him ?

Two days after the body of Betty Jane Kennedy was found, Hagerstown police had "established the fact that Miss Kennedy was last seen alive late Wednesday evening in Hagerstown, and (1) two men were looking for her Wednesday evening, (2) one of the men was heard to utter a threat of what he would do when he found her. One of the men is said to be a soldier." At the same time, Pennsylvania State Police noted that "there were neither footprints nor vehicle marks on the cinder-covered ground in the thickly wooded section" where Betty Kennedy had died.[17]

At the height of the Kennedy investigation, the City of Hagerstown accepted the resignation of Chief of Police Peters, who nevertheless remained on the force as a detective.[18] He continued to work on the Kennedy case.

On April 8, 1946, authorities detained the aforementioned cab driver after a Hagerstown dry cleaning establishment produced a pair of bloodstained trousers he had left with them for cleaning. The driver in question had been seen with Betty Jane Ken-

---

[17] "Break in Girl's Murder Seen as 2 Men Sought," *The Daily Mail* (Hagerstown, Md.), April 6, 1946, p. 1, col. 2. The two men who were searching for Miss Kennedy are believed to have been W. Edgar "Scrappy" Snider and Lawrence E. Speece, the latter supposedly the one who uttered the threat against Betty Jane.

[18] "Know Your Policeman," *The Daily Mail* (Hagerstown, Md.), October 29, 1946, p. 14, col. 6.

nedy on numerous occasions, but in particular on the evening of Wednesday, April 3.[19] The cab driver, who was married, lied continually during the investigation but nevertheless passed a polygraph test. His release occurred on April 10. He told investigators that the bloodstains were from a passenger's bloody nose.

On April 10, while hunting mushrooms, Maurice Monn, of Waynesboro, found a tan ladies' pump for the right foot, size 8-1/2, near the summer cottage of Mrs. Albert Pryor, along the Antietam (Glen Forney-Old Forge) road. The shoe's "outside was mud-stained, as though the wearer had been dragged, the heel was partially broken off and mud was caked between the sole and the heel of the pump. Marks gave evidence that the wearer might have been in a struggle. All this and the fact that the Kennedy girl's shoes are still missing, sent police on an extensive hunt into the mountains about the Old Forge and Beartown sections yesterday afternoon."[20]

Based on finding shoes Betty Jane Kennedy had left at her sister's house, Hagerstown police determined that Betty had worn a size 6 or 6-1/2 shoe. Despite the fact that the shoe found near Old Forge had part of a woman's slip stuffed into its toe (suggesting that it was too large for the wearer instead of "too small" as reported), investigators concluded that it had no connexion to the Kennedy case.[21]

At this time the police also were working the theory that an unknown person had slain Betty Kennedy and then paid a taxicab driver to dispose of the body. No leads ever developed along that line.[22]

On April 11, police revealed the missing items of Betty Kennedy's clothing: a red dress with white buttons, brassiere, stepins,[23] and shoes. In 1951, workmen either demolishing or renovating the Potomac Hotel in downtown Hagerstown supposedly found

---

[19] "Blood-Stained Trousers are Discovered," *The Record Herald* (Waynesboro, Pa.), April 8, 1946, p. 1, col. 8.

[20] "No Developments Yet in Kennedy Case," *The Record Herald* (Waynesboro, Pa.), April 11, 1946, p. 1.

[21] *Ibid.*

[22] *Ibid.*

[23] Panties.

a red dress and a few other related articles stuffed between a bathtub and a wall. The dress mysteriously vanished before policemen arrived on the scene. Despite a concentrated search including a lengthy canvass of a Washington county dump, authorities never recovered the dress.[24]

On April 12, Washington County Sheriff Huyett offered a reward of three hundred dollars from his own funds for information leading to the arrest of the party or parties responsible for Miss Kennedy's murder. The Washington County Commissioners followed suit by offering an additional one hundred dollars.[25]

On April 15, Mrs. Bernadine Toms found Betty Jane Kennedy's shoes in the underbrush approximately ten feet off Old Route 16, a mile and a half above the spot where the body had been found.[26]

Police investigators also found a length of rope not far from where Betty Kennedy was found dead, but never established whether it was the murder weapon.

On April 18, Deputy Spickler found a "cigarette lighter, mirror, compact and small gold trinket which Betty Jane Kennedy carried with her the last night she was seen alive" one hundred fifty yards from where her purse had been found. Spickler told newspapers that all of Miss Kennedy's possessions had been found on the same side of the highway where her body was found.[27]

After April 19, 1946, the Kennedy story began fading from the news. On August 26, 1946, Sergeant Hartman, Pennsylvania State Police, assured the public that his agency was still working the case. Hartman was convinced that the uniformed man with whom Betty Kennedy was last seen alive was a soldier stationed at Camp Ritchie, Maryland.[28] Hartman based his conclusion on several facts: First, the camp was a short distance from the site

---

[24] "5-Year Old Murder Mystery Reopens in Two State Area," *The Record Herald* (Waynesboro, Pa.), August 15, 1951, p. 1, col. 1. *See also* "Betty Jane Kennedy's murder still unsolved after 35 years," *The Record Herald* (Waynesboro, Pa.), April 4, 1981, p. 7.

[25] "Rewards Offered in Slaying of Local Girl; Shoes Found," *The Morning Herald* (Hagerstown, Md.), April 17, 1946, p. 1.

[26] "Girl's Shoes Recovered," *The Record Herald* (Waynesboro, Pa.), April 16, 1946, p. 1, col. 3.

[27] "More Accessories of Slain Girl Located," *The Morning Herald* (Hagerstown, Md.), April 19, 1946, p. 1.

[28] Later renamed "Fort Ritchie."

where the corpse was found. Second, Betty Kennedy's death by strangulation was precisely the type of killing taught at the Government Intelligence Center at Camp Ritchie during the Second World War. Finally, hundreds of intelligence officers who had been taught that sort of strangulation were stationed at Camp Ritchie at the time the murder occurred.[29]

In June 1946, Pennsylvania arrested James Charles Butts on a warrant from Maryland for robbery as well as nonsupport and desertion. Sergeant Hartman of the Pennsylvania State Police Criminal Division questioned Butts about the Kennedy murder, and was satisfied that Butts had not been involved in the slaying. Butts later waived extradition, and was returned to Maryland.[30]

Then, on her deathbed, a Beartown[31] woman who died October 14, 1946, told a physician and a constable that her husband and two other men had probably murdered Betty Jane Kennedy. This implicated "Scrappy" Snider and his friend Lawrence E. Speece, whom investigators had already interviewed and virtually eliminated as suspects. The gist of the confession was that Speece and a man from Virginia had come to visit Snider at his Beartown residence. The night that Betty Kennedy was last seen alive, Mrs. Snider alleged, Speece tied the girl to a chair in the Snider house and strangled her with a wire. When he released the girl, she ran screaming from the cabin. Snider and Speece pursued her, and when they returned to the Snider place they were alone. Another Beartown resident heard a woman scream on the same night.[32] "State Police discounted the story figuring the woman had read newspaper accounts and concocted the story," yet Constable Melvin F. Summers, who was quite familiar with the denizens of Beartown, claimed that the woman was illiterate.[33]

---

[29] "A bizarre mystery. . .," *The Record Herald* (Waynesboro, Pa.), April 3, 1974, p. 4, col. 6.

[30] "Suspect is Released in Kennedy Case," *The Record Herald* (Waynesboro, Pa.), June 27, 1946, p. 1, col. 7. *See also* "Suspect Being Questioned in Kennedy Case," *The Record Herald* (Waynesboro, Pa.), June 25, 1946, p. 1, col. 5.

[31] A settlement very near the site where Betty Jane Kennedy's body was found.

[32] "Reveal Death Bed Statement in Pennsy in Kennedy Murder," *The Daily Mail* (Hagerstown, Md.), June 12, 1947, p. 5, col. 3.

[33] "5-Year Old Murder Mystery Reopens in Two State Area," *supra,* and p. 2,

On November 21, 1946, Detective Sergeant Hartman and Hagerstown Police Detective Norman Wolfe eliminated a thirty-one-year-old former cook at the Maryland State Sanatorium from among their suspects in the Kennedy case. The cook, Donald Moeller, *alias* Nelson Moeller and George Wilson, had married a former Hagerstown girl one week beforehand, and was being held in Baltimore on suspicion of robbery. The detectives ascertained that Moeller had been elsewhere when the murder was committed.[34]

Almost four years after the murder, the incarcerated leader of a safecracking gang claimed on his deathbed that he and his associates had murdered Betty Jane because "she knew too much." This ignited renewed interest in the case. At this juncture, Detective Sergeant J. J. Cassidy of the Maryland State Police, his Pennsylvania counterpart Detective Sergeant Hartman, and Hagerstown detective William Peters worked the case. They questioned four men about the allegation that Miss Kennedy had been slain in a Hagerstown hotel. After her murder, the confession alleged, the murderers lowered the body by rope from a hotel window on the night of April 4, 1946, and loaded it into a waiting automobile. The confession alleged that the body was then driven to Pennsylvania and tossed from the car along a lonely stretch of Old Route 16. Ultimately the authorities announced that, although the investigation was still very much alive in both States, they had found nothing to support the new theory, and the suspects were released.[35]

Around the same time, the discovery of a red-haired woman's body discarded along a lonely road near Hancock, Maryland, raised the question whether the "Red-Head Murder" and the Kennedy slaying were connected. Only twenty-seven miles separated the two crime scenes.[36]

---

col. 5.

[34] "Former Cook Almost Eliminated as Murder Case Suspect," *The Record Herald* (Waynesboro, Pa.), November 21, 1946, p. 1, col. 1.

[35] "Was Betty Jane Kennedy Slain in a Local Hotel?" *The Morning Herald* (Hagerstown, Md.), October 5, 1950, p. 1; "Another Theory in Kennedy Slaying Mystery Explodes," *The Record Herald* (Waynesboro, Pa.), October 5, 1950, p. 1, col. 2.

[36] "Another," *The Record Herald* (Waynesboro, Pa.), October 5, 1950, p. 2, col. 4.

Finally, in 1984, police reopened the Kennedy case after receiving a strange telephone call. At that time, Lieutenant Matthew P. Hunt, commander of the Pennsylvania State Police substation at Chambersburg, noted, "Unsolved cases are never closed." Nothing substantial materialized during the renewed investigation. At that time, the Kennedy case was one of three unsolved murders in Franklin county.[37]

My first 2013 interview was with Pennsylvania State Police criminal investigator Sergeant Dick. He explained that the Kennedy case was no longer listed as "unsolved." He could offer no further information, nor would he help me. Following this wasted effort, I contacted Pennsylvania State Police Criminal Investigation Division, Harrisburg but received nothing helpful.

Detective Sergeant Bachtell, Maryland State Police, was my next interview. Although he was more helpful than his Pennsylvania counterpart, he told me that any information they had gathered would be in the State Archives at Annapolis. He further noted that, since the Maryland State Police were not the primary investigators in the case, he doubted their records would contain much information of help to the PSI investigation.

The Hagerstown Public Information Director told me they had lost all of their records when the basement of the old station flooded.

Although Sergeant Weaver of the Washington County Sheriff's Office spent the most time talking to me, he was unaware of the Kennedy case and thought he could not help me.

A Franklin County Sheriff's deputy said that that office was never involved in the Kennedy murder investigation.

Waynesboro police told me they knew nothing and had no time to talk to me.

The Frederick office of the Federal Bureau of Investigation told me to file a Freedom of Information Act request. They noted that what PSI would receive would depend on how much money I was willing to spend, and then there was no guarantee they would send me what I sought.

---

[37] "Tip revives '46 murder investigation," *The Record Herald* (Waynesboro, Pa.), April 19, 1984, p. 1, col. 5.

I had scheduled an interview with District Attorney Maxwell, but he passed away before we could talk.

Based on the foregoing herein presented, I have reached the following conclusions: (1) Betty Jane Kennedy knew her killer. (2) The motive was personal. (3) Police had the killer in custody and released him.

The 1946 murder of Miss Betty Jane Kennedy remains one of the great American unsolved mysteries. Because of the lack of cooperation the various law enforcement agencies have shown PSI, we must rely heavily on newspaper accounts for our analysis of the case. Fortunately, the Hagerstown and Waynesboro newspapers covered the matter thoroughly, and have published comprehensive retrospectives about the investigation, especially in the decade following the tragedy.[38]

One reporter for *The Record Herald*, Edward V. Koterba, using the *nom de plume* "Hank Hayseed," was particularly curious about why the Kennedy case had stumped the police. On the sixth anniversary of Betty Jane's death, he queried—

"Why hasn't the crime been solved ?

"There is good reason to believe that the investigation was bungled.

"Seven different investigative agencies had their fingers in the pot, some of them falling over themselves seeking the glory of 'breaking the case.'

"This uncoordinated system of investigation may well have been the factor which has give the murderer or murderers their freedom."[39]

PSI agrees. Not only was the investigation uncoordinated but

---

[38] *See* "Betty Jane Kennedy's murder still unsolved after 35 years," *supra*; "Who Strangled Betty Jane Kennedy ? Police Continue Investigation of Mystery," *The Record Herald* (Waynesboro, Pa.), April 3, 1947, p. 1, col. 3; "'Still Have High Hopes' of Solving the Kennedy Slaying, Police Declare," *The Record Herald* (Waynesboro, Pa.), April 2, 1949, p. 1, col. 4; "Betty Jane Kennedy Murder Case Still Baffles Authorities," *The Record Herald* (Waynesboro, Pa.), April 3, 1948, p. 1; "A bizarre mystery. . .," *supra*; "Kennedy Murder Case Remains Unsolved," *The Daily Mail* (Hagerstown, Md.), March 9, 1954, p. 5.

[39] "Kennedy Murder Case," *The Record Herald* (Waynesboro, Pa.), April 4, 1952, p. 6, col. 3.

unimaginative. Pennsylvania State Police and Hagerstown Police relied heavily on polygraph tests in deciding which suspects to detain or eliminate from suspicion—tests which are notoriously unreliable and inadmissible as evidence in court. The detectives also seem to have been preoccupied with the notion that Miss Kennedy's companion in uniform was stationed at Camp Ritchie. One of the prime suspects in the case, Lawrence E. Speece, of Ohio, was a deserter from the army at the time the murder occurred, but news reports from that era make no mention of his military status or of the possibility of his being the man in uniform. The focus on Camp Ritchie also stonewalled the investigation because of the massive amount of records through which Detective Sergeant Hartman of the Pennsylvania State Police would have needed to wade if he were to match a soldier's personnel records with the description of Miss Kennedy's last known associate, the tall, bronzed, handsome fellow with shiny black hair and a battle jacket loaded with ribbons.

Consequently, the second part of this case analysis will focus on the suspicion which fell on ex-convicts William Edgar Snider, Lawrence E. Speece, and their unidentified out-of-town acquaintance at the time the murder investigation was at its zenith.

PSI is still, in the words of Detective Sergeant Hartman, "working the case."

V.
Massacre of the Newey Household.

Timothy J. Shockey.

May 14, 2013.

Thirty-eight persons attended the fifth meeting of the Potomac Street Irregulars, which was held at the Parlor House. The evening's topic, the massacre of the John Newey household, is historically important because it resulted in the first execution for murder in Maryland based entirely on circumstantial evidence. So important were newspaper accounts in the resolution of this case, that the Editor has considered it fitting to quote many of them rather than summarize their contents and thus lose some of the poignancy they contain. Likewise, the story of a deathbed confession to the crimes, signed "Medicus," is restated verbatim, not because it deserves any great credence, but because it is entertaining and illustrates how the passage of thirty-five years can cloud one's memory of events.

URING the night of Wednesday, December 29, 1830, someone brutally killed everyone inside the dwelling house of John Newey on South Mountain in Frederick county, Maryland, and then set the house afire. A coroner's inquest determined that person or persons unknown had murdered the entire Newey household.

Suspicion for the crime immediately attached to a nephew of John Newey, one John Markley, because he had (1) a criminal record, (2) uttered terroristic threats against members of the Newey family, and (3) been seen in the vicinity of the Newey place shortly before the tragedy. Ultimately, a Frederick county jury convicted Markley of the murder of John Newey, and he was hanged at Frederick, Maryland, on June 24, 1831.[1]

Markley became the first person executed for murder in Maryland based entirely on circumstantial evidence. He protested his innocence to the very end of his life; and even though the whole world seemed prejudiced against him, some onlookers believed

---

[1] John Markley, a rough carpenter, was the illegitimate son of John Newey's sister.

him, especially many years later when someone else supposedly made a deathbed confession of the crime. Who, therefore, killed the Newey family?

Soon after the massacre occurred, the newspapers of nearby towns began reporting the crime with great indignation, inciting great hostility towards John Markley in the public mind before he was even captured. One of the Gettysburg papers had this to say:

> "We have this week to record one of the most horrible crimes that have [sic] ever darkened our columns; and one, which humanity would fain hope might prove exaggerated.
>
> "On Wednesday night last, the dwelling-house of Mr. Newey, in Harbaugh's valley, was burnt by fire, together with all its unfortunate inmates, Mr. Newey, his wife,[2] and two children,[3] Mr. Tressler,[4] (father of Mrs. Newey) and a bound body[5]—six in number!—Mrs. Newey was also far advanced in pregnancy!
>
> "Some of the neighbors having discovered the light, hastened to the spot; and although the house was so much on fire, as to prevent their entrance, a most horrid spectacle was fully exposed to their view. Mr. Newey was lying upon the floor dead, with his rifle under him, and a large hole in the side of his head; Mr. Tressler, and the bound boy, were also lying dead in different parts of the lower floor; Mrs. Newey was in her bed, which, with the garments she wore, was completed saturated with blood! The two children were also dead in their bed. The bodies of all were soon consumed by the raging flames, with the exception of that of Mrs. Newey, part of which the falling of the wall, and the quantity of blood, prevented from being entirely consumed. Two stabs were discovered in her body; and it is stated, the sculls of all were cleft.
>
> "Not a doubt exists in the mind of any one, but that the whole family were murdered, in the first place, and the house then set on fire to conceal the horrid deed! A coroner's inquest reported them murdered by some villain or villains unknown.

---

[2] *Nee* Lydia Tressler.

[3] Miss Sera Miller, of Solomon's Island, Md., has thoroughly researched the Newey massacre and the families who were neighbours of the Neweys. She offers the names of the children, Elizabeth and Daniel, and cites Maryland State Archives T176-69 Box 86 01/42/13/006 for her authority. This refutes the common belief that the children were two girls named Ruth and Ann.

[4] Jacob Tressler.

[5] John Coombs.

"Strong suspicions are afloat as to the perpetrators, but we have not heard of any arrests, as yet."[6]

The news reporting was not necessarily as accurate as it was sensational, as the initial report of another Gettysburg sheet attests:

"HORRID MURDERS.—A shocking scene was exhibited on Thursday night last, at the residence of Mr. *John Newey*, in Harbaugh's Valley, Frederick county, Md. About 5 miles from Millerstown,[7] in this county. Mr. Newey and all his family are supposed to have been murdered, and the house then set on fire. The family consisted of 6 (or, rather 7) persons, viz. Mr. Newey, his father-in-law named Jacob Tressler, Mrs. Newey, and three children, (one unborn,) and a bound boy, about 17 or 18 years of age named Patrick Lafferty. Two or three persons who first arrived at the fire, saw that Mr. Newey's head was broken; after alarming the neighborhood, the chief exertions were made to save the bed on which Mrs. Newey lay—in which they partly succeeded, and found the bed very bloody. The body of Mr. Tressler was all consumed except the bones; that of Lafferty about half, and the others roasted and crisped in a shocking manner. Mr. Newey's rifle lay under his body on the floor.

"The perpetrators are suspected to be two men named *King*, and *Nicholas*. They had been sent to the Maryland penitentiary for robbing Mr. Newey, a few years since; had used threatening language since their liberation, and left the neighborhood on the night of the murder."[8]

The *Compiler* quickly corrected its errors:

"There were several errors in our notice of the murder of the family of Mr. Newey, published last week. The distance from Millerstown is ten or eleven miles—or about 18 or 19 from this place. The name of the person on whom the principal suspicion rests, is *John Markle*, (not King)—a nephew of Mr. Newey, and step-son of Mr. King. The name of the bound boy was *J. Coombs*, not Patrick Lafferty. It was the falling of the materials of the wall upon it, that partly saved the body of Mrs. Newey from being burnt. She had been twice stabbed in the Stomach.—This appears to be an affair

---

[6] "Horrible!" *The Adams Sentinel* (Gettysburg, Pa.), January 4, 1831, p. 4.
[7] Now Fairfield, Adams county, Pa.
[8] *Gettysburg Compiler* (Gettysburg, Pa.), p. 3.

something like that of White and the Knapps,[9] in Massachusetts—as the persons suspected of perpetrating and being accessory to the horrid transaction, are all nephews or other relatives of Mr. Newey, who now become heirs to his property."[10]

The Frederick-Town Herald reported the Newey massacre with a literary flourish and some venom for John Markley, who had yet to be convicted of Newey's murder:

"MOST HORRIBLE !!! The most horrible tragedy enacted in Harbaugh's valley, the particulars of which we give from the 'Examiner,' has caused an awful sensation in our community. When contemplating it, 'tis difficult to believe that human nature can become so debased, or that revenge would call for so many victims; and we exclaim with McDuff—'What *all*—all hell-kite!' The perpetrator still walks in darkness, but we trust the strong arm of justice will soon bring him forth to the light—escape he cannot, for there are 'miraculous organs' which will proclaim his guilt, bide where he may.

"John Markley, the individual suspected of the horrid crime, was tried in Frederick county court on the 26th October, 1825, and convicted of stealing from Mr. John Newey, bank notes, two watches, and other articles valued in the aggregate at $194 75 cents;—for which he was sentenced to five years confinement.—He is now 38 years of age; in height five feet 11¾ inches, has dark complexion, and dark hair, stoops somewhat in walking, but is well proportioned, and stoutly made.

"In addition to the facts detailed below, we have been informed that the body of Mrs. Newey has been disenterred [*sic*], and if any doubt remained as to the manner of her death, they have been removed by a re-examination of it and the garments she wore at the time of the catastrophe.

"On Wednesday night last, 29th Dec. a Mr. NEWEY, who lived in Harbaugh's Valley, in this county,[11] was murdered, together with his *wife, two children, father-in-law, and an apprentice boy*, and the house was afterwards set on fire and consumed. The circumstances

---

[9] In 1830, John Francis Knapp and Joseph Jenkins Knapp were convicted and executed at Salem, Mass., for the clubbing and stabbing murder of their uncle Captain Joseph White.

[10] *Gettysburg Compiler*, January 11, 1831, p. 3, col. 1.

[11] The location of the Newey house was near the present Sabillasville, on the south side of Fort Ritchie road, between its intersections with Skunk Hollow and Raven Rock roads, on lands now owned by Mrs. Buhrman. Only some foundation stones remain to mark the spot where the Newey household perished.

attending its discovery are these: On Thursday morning last, Mr. Flaut,[12] who lives about 400 yards from the house of Mr. Newey, with woods intervening, was surprised on rising to find a dark cloud over the house of his neighbour; and, his suspicions being awakened by the unusual appearance of the atmosphere, he sent a lad to ascertain if any thing were the matter, who soon returned and reported that the house was burnt, and the inmates probably consumed with it, as none could be seen. On repairing thither, our informant found Mr. Newey lying on the floor, nearly consumed, with his rife by his side; Mrs. Newey, partly consumed, with stabs in several places; the two children, partly consumed, with the bedclothes under them wet with their blood; and the old man and the boy both consumed.—Appearances seemed to indicate that the wife, sleeping in front, was first stabbed; that the husband, on reaching for his rifle, was prostrated by a blow with an axe and killed; that the two children were killed in bed; that the father-in-law, who, with the lad, slept in a chamber above, on coming down to ascertain the noise, was killed as he entered the room; and that the boy, after coming down, had nearly succeeded in making his way to the door, which opened to the road, when he was struck down.

"By whom the murder was committed is not known. Suspicion, however, strongly fastens upon one Markley, the nephew of Mr. Newey, who, five years since, was sentenced by Frederick county court to imprisonment in the penitentiary for stealing from Mr. Newey a wedding suit of clothes, a watch and $250.—At that time Mr. Newey had just been married. The time for which Markley was sentenced to the penitentiary expired, we believe, on the 25th of November last. After his conviction, and whilst in the penitentiary, he made threats of vengeance against his uncle. Another nephew of Mr. Newey, who was sentenced at the same time, perhaps for the same offence, and whose time expired last fall, gave intimations to Mr. Newey to beware of Markley.

"It is supposed the crime was perpetrated by more than one. The person of Markley is known to but few in the vicinity—to but one, it is believed, (the nephew of Mr. Newey's wife,) who was evidence against Markley at his trial, and who is likewise included in that wretch's denunciations."[13]

The *Repository* chimed in from Franklin county: "Mr. Newey was known to have had a considerable sum of money in his house (some say 1000 and others between 4 & 500 dollars) which the

---

[12] Captain George Flautt, a justice of the peace and militia officer in Frederick county, Md. He died in Perry county, O., on November 28, 1862.

[13] *The Frederick-Town Herald* (Frederick, Md.), January 8, 1831, p. 3.

wretches no doubt secured before they set fire to the house."[14]
The *Baltimore Patriot* reported Markley's arrest:

> "We learn that *John Marklay*, who has recently been discharged
> from a five years term at the Maryland Penitentiary, and on whom
> suspicion rested as being concerned in the late murder in Har-
> baugh's Valley—was last evening apprehended in this city by Mr.
> *W. Walker* and two or three of our citizens, and after an examination
> by James Blair, esq. was committed for further examination, before
> whom he will be brought on Saturday next at 10 o'clock. He denied
> having ever been either in a Gaol or State-prison, but on entering
> our prison was immediately recognised by one of the keepers of the
> Penitentiary, who happened to be there, as the same Marklay de-
> scribed by the Frederick Citizen. On Friday night week he slept at
> Westminster, and on the following day arrived in Baltimore.
>
> "The account he gave of himself since the murder of the Newey
> family and burning of their dwelling, was contradictory throughout.
> Marklay is a powerful, broad-shouldered, athletic man, and answers
> the description heretofore given of him. There was found upon him
> a $10 Chambersburg note and a quantity of new clothing."[15]

Markley was indeed subjected to further examination before
'Squire Blair, as reported in the *Patriot*:

> "*Further Examination.—Markley* was further examined on Sat-
> urday last before *J. Blair*, esq. In the course of which, some of the
> clothing of Newey (the deceased) found in the possession of Mark-
> ley, was identified by one of the witnesses from Frederick county;
> this, and other corroborating circumstances, leave but little doubt
> that Markley and his accomplice (who is stated to be a stout, good
> looking, intelligent fellow, fair complexion, sandy hair and whis-
> kers, and about 5 feet 10 or 11 inches high, and is supposed to have
> accompanied Markley to Baltimore after the murder) are the per-
> sons who committed the horrid outrage.[16]
>
> "Markley was seen the day before the murder and arson were
> committed, within two miles of Newey's dwelling, and made en-
> quiry whether he still resided in the same place, threatning [*sic*]

---

[14] *The Torch Light & Public Advertiser* (Hagerstown, Md.), January 13, 1831,
p. 2.

[15] *Ibid.*

[16] Christian Frydinger was later arrested on suspicion of being Markley's
accomplice; however, the examining magistrate discharged Frydinger because
there was no evidence against him. *The Adams Sentinel* (Gettysburg, Pa.), July
19, 1831, p. 5.

that he would destroy the whole family, and then give himself up to be hung. On the night after, Markley and his companion staid in Smith's town, distant six miles from Newey's house; they sat up all night and departed by day break in the morning. He was re-committed and will be delivered to the Sheriff of Frederick county, preparatory to his trial."[17]

One of the most damaging pieces of evidence for Markley was a pair of John Newey's pantaloons which, because of a fanciful mending job, were unique. Markley's possession of these pantaloons and some other items of Newey's property seemed unexplainable except for his having stolen them when committing the crimes—until an old gentleman's deathbed confession purported to explain how the stuff was "planted" on Markley, as hereinafter set forth.

The Frederick-Town Herald gave another perspective of Markley's "further examination":

"Examination of Markley. We have conversed with Mr. *King*, the gentleman who went to Baltimore to attend the examination of *Markley*, which took place on Saturday last, and his statements would induce a belief that Markley is one of the party which committed the murders. Mr. King has known Markley for a long time, and was one of the witnesses on whose testimony he was sentenced to five years imprisonment in the penitentiary,—but, on being confronted with Mr. *K.* he pretended that he did not know him or Mr. Newey, and said that he had not been in Frederick county for ten years.

"Among the clothing of Mr. Newey, there was a pair of pantaloons of a peculiar make, of velvet, that were too short for him, and which had been torn or ripped on one side, near the pocket, and sewed up with *white thread.* This pair of pantaloons Mr. King had seen Mr. Newey frequently wear, and had often joked with him on their singular appearance—and at one time was about purchasing them. On being asked by the magistrate if he recollected Mr. Newey's clothing, he described correctly the pantaloons above mentioned, and on examining Markley's bundle a pair of pantaloons of precisely the same materials &c. were discovered! *which Mr. King made oath were Mr. Newey's property.* In Markley's bundle there were other articles of clothing, which Mr. King thinks will be identified by the neighbors, as belonging to Mr. Newey's family.

[17] *Ibid.*, January 20, 1831, p. 2.

"There was also in the bundle about a *yard and half* of calico with large *cross bars of yellow and green,* which it is thought may have been purchased of store-keepers in the neighborhood, in consequence of Mrs. Newey's 'peculiar situation'—a specimen has been left with us, and store-keepers, residing in the late Mr. Newey's neighborhood, are invited to call and examine it. We are further informed by Mr. King, that Markley stated where he was on every night except that on which the murder was committed—but of that night he could give no account.

" * * * "[18]

In February 1831, John Markley was moved from Baltimore to Frederick, to be tried at the May 1831 term of criminal court.[19] As the prosecution and defense counsel prepared their cases, the press continued its intense coverage of Markley's case as well as their premature conviction of him for the murders and arson committed in the mountains. With not one whit of regard for the presumption of innocence, one otherwise sophisticated writer visited the Frederick county jail to catch a glimpse of the accused, and then waxed poetic in his self-righteous condemnation of the wayward rustic:

"MARKLEY—*The Murderer.*

This is the bloodiest shame,
The wildest savagery, the vilest stroke,
That ever wall-eyed wrath or staring rage
Presented to the tears of soft remorse.
King John.

"I had lately an occasion to visit Fredericktown—and having heard that *Markley* had recently been confined to the county Jail, I resolved to get a view of him. I was conducted into a room where there were several malefactors assembled around the stove—and although I had never seen Markley before, I immediately distinguished him from the other criminals. He was, in the language of the great dramatist,

'A fellow by the hand of nature mark'd,
Quoted and sign'd, to do a deed of shame.'

---

[18] *The Frederick-Town Herald,* January 22, 1831, p. 3.
[19] *The Adams Sentinel* (Gettysburg, Pa.), February 15, 1831, p. 7.

"He is a man of the most athletic and vigorous frame—his head is large, exhibiting the 'organ of destructiveness' very prominently developed.—His forehead is shaded by a profusion of dark bushy hair—an unrelenting frown darkens his brow, and the lines of his countenance exhibit the most diabolical passions. But no pen can describe the cruel expression of his dark eye, when some horrid feeling agitates his mind. The deadly glance of the tiger, when he is about to spring upon his prey, would convey the best idea of the malignant feeling which appears to characterize it.

"Some five or six years ago, Markley was condemned to hard labor in the Baltimore Penitentiary, for a term of years. The principal evidence against him was Mr. Newey, his uncle. From the moment that his sentence was pronounced, he seems to have harbored projects of implacable vengeance against his intended victim. He was heard, whilst in confinement, frequently making threats, but these were disregarded—and when his term was out, he was discharged. Having furnished himself with what was necessary for his purpose, he secretly repaired to his uncle's house, situated in the midst of a solitary heath, and concealed himself till the family were asleep. He entered the bed room, and was first observed by his aunt, who uttered a scream. He stabbed her. Newy [*sic*] rose from his bed and grasped his rifle—but before he could use it, he was felled to the ground by the ruffian, who despatched him with an axe. There were two children asleep in the bed. What could have induced him to bathe his hands in their innocent blood? If he had spared them, his name would not have been loaded with the execrations which have since pursued him. But he was actuated by the furies! —He stabbed those harmless victims, and barbarously mangled their naked bodies. To leave no trace of his crime, he set fire to the house and then wandered away like Cain, with the murderer's mark upon him.

"Since the arrest of this monster, some suspicions have been revived, that he was the violator and assassin of Miss Cunningham, whose tragical fate will no doubt recur to the reader's memory. Soon after the perpetration of that crime, he was arrested—but released for want of sufficient testimony.—He may possibly have been innocent of that horrible outrage; but whoever was the guilty person, must have been one who had a heart to conceive, and a hand to execute, barbarities of no common character—such for instance, as the massacre of the Newey family which I have just recorded.

"DESIDERIUS."[20]

---

[20] "Extract from a communication in the Washington City Chronicle," *The Torch Light & Public Advertiser*, April 14, 1831, p. 1.

John Markley was indeed suspected in the murder of Miss Evelina Cunningham, in Cecil county, Maryland, in 1825. There was, however, insufficient evidence to prosecute him for that crime. One Peters, *alias* John Connors, was subsequently tried and acquitted of the crimes against Miss Cunningham, and in 1834, one George Stebbing, a shoemaker, was tried and acquitted. The general sentiment nevertheless was that Stebbing, who dwelt near the scene of Miss Cunningham's murder, was in fact guilty.[21]

The totality of the newspaper items about the Cunningham and Newey murders shows that journalists of the early Nineteenth century sometimes assumed that persons merely accused of crimes were guilty of the same. This not only resulted, no doubt, in miscarriages of justice, but has also muddied the waters for such present-day investigators as the Potomac Street Irregulars. The press was particularly hard on John Markley. Shortly after the murder of Miss Cunningham, *The Maryland Gazette* copied this item from the Harper's Ferry *Free Press*:

"LOOK OUT FOR THE MURDERER!

"A man of a suspicious appearance and character has been in Loudoun county, near Harper's Ferry, for a week past, and a strong belief has been excited, from a variety of circumstances, that he is the murderer of Miss Cunningham, near Baltimore. He answers the description of the monster, given in the newspapers, except as to dress, which he says he lost with his knapsack in Newmarket, Md. He afterwards, however, engaged a washerwoman, stating that he intended in a few days to go for his clothes. He returned to the Loudon [*sic*] settlement on Tuesday, the 19th instant, having been absent since the 1st of March—He informed Mr. Shriver, a respectable citizen of Loudon, that he passed by the place about two hours after the murder! He was the first who gave Mr. S. information of it, and conversed about it in a manner which betrayed some anxiety or uneasiness. He was much disturbed in his sleep, frequently exclaiming—'There they are! there! there! don't you seem them? look at her! look at her! She's a beautiful girl! Poor thing, she's dead! Where's the child?'" When awakened, and questioned on

---

[21] *See The Torch Light & Public Advertiser,* June 7, 1825, p. 2, June 21, 1825, p. 2, and July 27, 1826, p. 4; *The Maryland Gazette* (Annapolis, Md.), July 14, 1825, p. 3; and *Tarboro' Press* (Tarboro, N. C.), May 9, 1834, p. 1.

the subject, he said that whether awake or asleep he continually saw a young woman, that he felt much disturbed and didn't know the cause of it, &c.

"As soon as he heard that a suspicion was excited, he disappeared. Several persons were in pursuit of him yesterday, and he was last heard of within a mile of Harper's Ferry, on the Maryland side.—His name is Markle; he has worked at this place, was convicted of theft in this county about 18 months since, and served 12 months in the penitentiary.

"Accompanying the extra sheet was a note from a gentleman stating that he had received it at Harper's Ferry—that he saw the man in gaol at Charlestown, Jefferson county, Va. Who told him he never was in Cecil—'but (adds the writer) I am inclined to think he is the criminal—This being published in your paper will apprise the friends of the young lady in Cecil.' Am."[22]

The Hagerstown paper updated readers on the quest to pin the Cunningham murder on John Markley, and announced John Newey's complaint against his nephew for burglarizing the Newey house:

"Harpers-Ferry, March 4.

"On Thursday last a man named JOHN MARKLEY was arrested in this neighborhood on suspicion of being the murderer of Miss *Evelina Cunningham*, near Baltimore, and of having assisted in the robbery of the house of *John Newey*, of Fred'k county, Md. As to his guilt on the last charge, there is scarcely room for a doubt; and during his examination on the first, he gave so many contradictory answers, and told so many palpable falsehoods, as to leave impressions highly unfavorable to him upon the minds of those who were present. He said he was in Baltimore at the time of the murder, but had previously informed one person at least that he had passed by the place of the murder *two hours after* it was comt'd. He is a person nearly 6 feet high, stoop-shouldered, has black hair & whiskers, and, says he is 33 years of age. He was 12 months in the penitentiary of this state. That he has been guilty of some crime, is evident from the perturbation of mind exhibited by him previous to his arrest; and the supposition is confirmed by the fact, that when he left Loudoun, on the 6th of March, he was nearly destitute of clothing, whereas when he returned, on the 18th of April, he had on a good suit of blue cloth, a hat nearly new, a fine shirt & waistcoat, boots not half worn. And yet, according to his own confession, he had

---

[22] *The Maryland Gazette* (Annapolis, Md.), May 5, 1825, p. 2.

not worked a day during his absence. He is now in Charlestown jail, awaiting a further examination. If the murderer has not been elsewhere detected, we hope the proper authorities in Maryland will take immediate measures to have an examination made of the person above named. *Free Press.*[23]

After the newspapers had managed to poison the community's consciousness against Markley with sensational, prejudicial statements, this item actually appeared in several local sheets:

"The trial of Markley, which is to take place, precludes the possibility of saying any thing which might have a tendency to prejudice his case; but the following, which has been related to us, has interest, and is the subject of common conversation:—Mr. Charles Smith, of Waynesburg, was lately in Baltimore, where he was shown a $10 note taken from Markley, which he identified as one that he had given to the late Mr. Newey. He knew it because, when Mr. Newey demurred about taking it, he wrote his own name on the back of it, and took a memorandum of the number."[24]

At all events, on Wednesday, May 18, 1831, the trial of John Markley opened in Frederick county, Chief Justice Buchanan presiding. He faced two indictments: one for the murder of John Newey, and one for the murder of Lydia Newey. The trial covered only the murder of John Newey. James Dixon appeared for the State, and William Ross and Joseph Palmer appeared for Markley. Acting on suggestions from both counsels, the court decided upon the following questions for prospective jurors:

1. "Have you formed and expressed an opinion as to the guilt or innocence of the accused?"

2. "Do you think, notwithstanding the reports you have heard, that you could give to the prisoner an impartial trial?"

3. Whether each juror "had conscientious scruples about convicting in a case of life and death on circumstantial testimony alone."

---

[23] *The Torch Light & Public Advertiser*, May 10, 1825, p. 2.
[24] "From the Fredericktown Examiner," *The Torch Light & Public Advertiser*, February 3, 1831, p. 4. At the time of the Newey murders, Charles Smith was a leading merchant of what is now Waynesboro, Franklin county, Pa.

These interrogatories were, of course, of paramount importance, because the press had already convicted Markley, and there was no direct evidence of his participation in Newey's murder.

After opening statements, in which the defense revealed it would not be calling witnesses, testimony commenced. George Flautt was the first witness. He testified, in part, as follows:

> "In the morning [of Thursday, December 30] I called up my boys early, a few hours before day—when my wife arose from bed she looked out of the window, and remarked that there was a great smoke over towards Newey's—One of my boys run down & returned upon one of Mr. Newey's horses & told us the house was on fire & he saw no one about it. I went down—the house was all on fire—we had a good view of all the inside of the house, and saw Newey lying on the floor with his feet towards the bed and his head towards the door—the hair was burnt off of his head and the skull and skin appeared quite white, and on the right side of his head there was a hole—it appeared to have been done with an axe. The skull was broken in—there were small cracks from the main wound like the cracks of an egg shell. I examined it particularly, as I expected I would have to testify on the subject."

Flautt's examination also revealed that, by the time other neighbors arrived on the scene, Newey's head was completely burnt to ashes. Flautt saw Mrs. Newey's body lying upon the downstairs bed, her head completely burnt off. He enumerated the persons believed to have been burnt in the house; that Mrs. Newey's body had been stabbed several times, and that he had heard that Mr. Newey had been warned to be on his guard against Markley.

The second witness was George Flautt's son John. He was at the fire fifteen minutes before his father. Then he mounted one of Newey's horses and returned home. He had not seen Newey's body upon his first trip to the scene. He noted that the house seemed to have been set on fire at both its top and its bottom.

A SOLITARY HOMESTEAD.

James Manahan and Daniel Benchoff were at the disinterment of Mrs. Newey's remains, and testified to the manner in which the rents in her linens matched up with the stab wounds in her body. Manahan put his fingers into the wounds and found that they were quite deep.

As for the threats Markley had made: John King testified that he heard Markley state, after his conviction for burglarizing the Newey place, that he would "have revenge." John Williams had been present at the jail when Markley was sentenced for the Newey burglary. He quoted Markley as saying, "If I ever get out, I will have satisfaction if I have to kill and burn up the whole of them."

John Black, who lived four miles from Emmitsburg, Maryland, on the turnpike road leading to Waynesburg, Pennsylvania, testified that Markley, calling himself 'Markell,' had stopped at his house on December 21, 1830, and spent the night. He had no knapsack, and left without paying Black.

Bernard Wright, of Smith's Town, Washington county, Maryland, positively identified Markley as the man who, on the first Friday after Newey's murder, about sunset, visited his house, seven miles from Newey's. At this juncture, Markley did have a knapsack, well filled with clothing. He and his companion told Wright that they came from Huntingdon county, Pennsylvania, and were going to travel down the New Cut road toward Frederick. When Markley paid him, Wright was astonished to see that his purse was the very same one which John Newey had used when he was at Wright's house about two weeks beforehand.

Joshua Kelly, of Baltimore, likewise positively identified the prisoner. He testified that Markley arrived at his tavern in Baltimore on January 2, 1831. He had plenty of money with which to pay his bar tab, and inquired about the price for boarding by the week. He noticed the stranger had a ten-dollar note on the Chambersburg bank. While Markley was there, the news of the Newey massacre reached Kelly's establishment. Markley was arrested while absent from the tavern, and never returned. His large bundle, tied up in a shawl, had remained in Kelly's possession.

John W. Walker, of Baltimore, was the officer who arrested John Markley. He sat with him at Kelly's tavern and made inquiry as to his place of residence, occupation, and business in Baltimore. Markley's answers were contradictory, and he denied having any relatives named "Newey." When Markley rose as if to leave, Walker also rose, and arrested him. Markley went peacefully but protested his innocence. At first, he denied ever having been in the penitentiary or in jail; however, after a turnkey recognized him, he confessed to having been there and implored the jailer to say that he had behaved well while held there.

Persons present at the preliminary examinations of Markley testified as to the particular contents of his bundle when he was taken into custody in Baltimore. Sally Manahan, Benchoff, and King positively identified several pieces of clothing as having belonged to Newey. One Mr. Tressler indicated that one of the vests which Markley had been carrying with him looked like one the Coombs boy had had.

In all, upwards of twenty witnesses testified. They established that John Newey had indeed been murdered, that Markley had threatened to get revenge against the Neweys, that the prisoner was Newey's nephew John Markley, and that items of clothing in his knapsack when he was arrested were definitely Newey's clothing.

After closing arguments, the jury retired for approximately half an hour. Thereupon they returned to the courtroom with a verdict of GUILTY OF MURDER IN THE FIRST DEGREE.[25]

On Sunday, May 29, 1831, Markley was summoned to court to hear the sentence to be imposed on him: death by hanging. Now that Markley was condemned, the press was not quite so harsh in its description of him. One Frederick newspaper noted in him the—

"same unperturbed aspect which had marked his features during the trial, and through the period of his confinement, the same appar-

---

[25] *The Frederick-Town Herald,* May 21, 1831, p. 2. *See also* Mrs. Frank Stough Schwartz (Harry D. Bowman, ed.), *The Flautt Family in America* (Hagerstown, Md.: Dixie Press, 1971), pp. 95*ff.*; *Republican Compiler* (Gettysburg, Pa.), May 31, 1831, p. 1.

ent insensibility to the wretchedness of his condition, was as strik-
ingly manifested on this solemn and impressive occasion. While
the crowd around him seemed deeply affected by a contemplation
of his forlorn and miserable situation, his countenance betrayed no
marks of an agitated mind or disturbed heart, but indicated more
the calmness and composure of an indifferent spectator to a less
melancholy scene. Neither was there, on the contrary, discoverable
in his countenance, at any time, the least fierceness of expression
or line of violent passion; but rather exhibited an habitually smooth
quiet temper."[26]

John Markley was hanged at Frederick between ten and elev-
en o'clock on Friday morning, June 24, 1831, in the presence of
thousands of onlookers. He protested his innocence even under
the gallows; the widespread rumor that he had confessed to the
murders was untrue. His body was given to scientists for dissec-
tion.[27]

≫≫≫≫●≪≪≪≪

One might think that that was the end of the saga. But in 1867
the Cincinnati *Commercial* ran an item submitted by a physician
using the *nom de plume* "Medicus," which newspapers across the
nation copied in their own pages. The story consisted of a fairly
loose recountal of the facts of the Markley case, the revelation of
another man's deathbed confession to the crime, and a lecture on
the evils of executing prisoners based solely on circumstantial
testimony. Regardless of its probity, this odd tale is so interesting, so compelling, that it is here repeated in its entirety:

"A STRANGE STORY.

"Every man is interested in the faithful administration of the
law, and every case in which its full vigor has been expended,
should be carefully scrutinized; as when life is taken no remedy
is left the State, and no reparation can be made. Markley was

---

[26] *The Torch Light & Public Advertiser,* June 2, 1831, p. 2 (quoting the *Freder-ick-Town Citizen*).
[27] "A Bit of History About the Execution of Markley," *The Gettysburg Times* (Gettysburg, Pa.), March 14, 1959, p. 6; *Gettysburg Compiler,* July 19, 1831, p. 2.

executed at Frederick City, Maryland, in the summer of 1830 [*sic*], for the murder of seven persons—his uncle, aunt, and three children, and his aunt's father and mother [*sic*]. His guilt was so clearly established that no man in a populous city and county doubted it; yet upon the gallows, and for days before the execution, he persisted in his innocence. The execution was public, in the presence of a large concourse of citizens. The attending clergyman, after the rope was adjusted, returned to the platform three times, and each time received the same answer—"I never murdered them, nor do I know who did."

"This answer was made known to the crowd each time, and not one human being present but was convinced that, to special cruelty was added a stolidity and stubbornness never before manifested by man. His body was given to the surgeons as soon as removed from the gallows, and in an adjacent barracks was publicly dissected, in the presence of a number of physicians and medical students, (of whom the writer was one,) and the entire day was given to anatomical demonstrations, by medical gentlemen selected for the purpose. No man objected, no friends asked for the body, and but one human being on earth then lived who knew Markley was innocent, and he was silent then, but an important witness during the trial. No man will doubt the fairness of that trial, when I mention the fact that Judges Buchanan and Shriver presided, and that the bar of Frederick was second to none in the Union. James Dixon, Esq. was prosecutor, and the Scleighs [*sic*] were the attorneys for the defense. The jury did not leave the box, and in the sentence Chief Justice Buchanan, with tears, asserted his full assent to the verdict of guilty, and said that in a long life he had not heard of so atrocious a case.

"We will now detail preliminaries, and give the testimony of one witness, from whose statements there could be but one conclusion, and that of guilty. The prisoner was an orphan, and by the Court was bound to his uncle for a term of year, in the usual manner, to receive a certain education, and at his majority, to have a certain sum of money. The boy was indisposed to go to school, and was idle; but was not regarded as vicious.

"Living in the country, and in a family where every moral duty was illustrated, and where kindness was the ruling element, he had nearly completed his apprenticeship, without any special objection being formed by his uncle or aunt, and possibly had not the loss of thirty-five dollars been discovered and traced to the boy, all would have gone on well until he would have fulfilled the time of his indentures. This was the youth's only offense, and after a full confession was heartily forgiven, and as far as the family knew, the fact was confined to themselves, and almost forgotten. By means as yet unknown, the fact became known, and the uncle was summoned before the grand jury, and compelled to testify to the truth, and in despite of his entreaties that the affair should be regarded as a youthful indiscretion, a true bill for larceny was found, the boy arrested and thrown into jail, and convicted and sentenced to the penitentiary for three years.

"He was taken to the penitentiary, and notwithstanding the most solemn assurances of his uncle and aunt, that they were not culpable in the exposure, and deeply sympathizing with him in his punishment, he believed they were not sincere, and said it was done to avoid the payment of his 'freedom money.' He regarded them as his worst enemies, and as they were the only witnesses, swore to be avenged upon his discharge from prison.

"His uncle could not make him comprehend the duty of a witness, and parted from him in tears, not more from the disgrace of the boy than from the sorrow that he should feel as he did toward a family whose hearts bled at the misfortune of their relative. Anxious to disabuse his mind, he visited the prisoner and returned, sorrowing that his nephew should, even after time should have mollified his feelings, still hold him responsible, and to the last threaten his life and that of his entire family. He would be revenged, and it should be summary and sure. So frequently before his confinement in the penitentiary were these threats made, as to be known to many persons and to every man from his neighborhood, who was permitted by the rules of the prison to visit Markley, heard from him the same threats, and spoke of them publicly. If the uncle ever entertained fears, he never spoke of them, and time passed to the completion of the term of the nephew's sentence, when immediately thereafter, on a Saturday [*sic*] night, the uncle's house was discovered on fire, and before any help could arrive, was burned with the entire contents. No soul was left alive to tell the sad tale of their deaths, and on examination of their charred remains, every one was found with their skull's [*sic*] cleft. This left no room to doubt that the entire family had been murdered, and the house burned to conceal the fact. In a community where crime was almost unknown, every member was on the alert to discover the murderer, and the threats of young Markley had their potential significance.

"His dismissal from prison was ascertained; more than that, he was seen in the vicinity of the farm but two days before the fire, and after an inquest, the Governor offered a reward of one thousand dollars, and bills were posted describing the supposed murderer. No means were left untried. Baltimore was patroled [*sic*], and orders given that every vessel leaving for foreign or coast trade should be overhauled, and yet without avail. Special police visited other States; cities were placarded with descriptions, and individuals joined the State and county in swelling the reward to such sums as called on hundreds to quit ordinary avocations, and turn special attention to hunting the murderer. The South Mountain was near the farm of the uncle. Old hunters who had hunted foxes and catamounts, explored caves and caverns, never before visited by man. All failed, and for three years [*sic*] the search was diligently prosecuted. So great a crime had, perhaps, never been committed in the State. Meetings in every county and large cities in the State were held, and the executor of the estate of the uncle offered as there was no immediate heirs, the entire farm for the discovery of the murderer, and no one doubted who he was. Three years thus passed, when news reached the settlement that young Markley had been arrested, down on the North Carolina coast near Ocracoke Inlet, where he had been for three years engaged in fishing. Perhaps no class of human beings are more depraved and secluded than the fisherman of the coast. Early in February the shad approached the coast, and from then until May are caught in large numbers, by men who have no earthly ties, and know no homes but their huts, and spend their leisure in drinking. But few survive two years, yet this healthy young man was in his third year of dissipation and exposure, and survived. How he was identified was never known. He was brought to Frederick city and placed in jail. He admitted that he saw the house on fire, but denied any knowledge of the deaths, or the causes of them. At the next session of the court he was indicted for the murder of seven [*sic*] persons, and the trial was short, proofs conclusive, and sentence followed.

"Before proceeding further I must introduce the principal witness, a young lady named Susan. She was raised by the family, and was not related to them, the child of a dear friend of the aunt, and was an orphan. She had grown to womanhood without feeling her orphanage or dependence, and was more an equal and companion of Mrs. Markley [sic] than a dependent. Her hand was solicited in marriage by several young men, and so importunately as a widower named P——, who owned the adjoining farm, and between whom and Mr. Markley [sic] there had been a law-suit involving the title to a mountain lot of wood, and the suit resulted in favor of Mr. Markley [sic]. Except this suit there was known no cause of disagreement between these neighbors, and the grown children of Mr. P., visited the Markleys [sic] after the suit as before, the father never, yet he embraced every opportunity to address Susan. She declined his addresses as she did others, alleging she would never quit the home where she found those as near and dear as her own father and mother, and as now the cares of children were added to the anxieties attendant upon the increasing years Mrs. Markley's parents (living with them), she could not think of deserting aunt, as she called Mrs. M. Such was Susan, and such was the relation between her and the Markley [sic] family.

"She appeared in court in the deepest mourning and although three years had elapsed—the presence of the supposed murderer—the recollection of past scenes and the horrid murder of those who were more than parents—her all in the world, so overcame her, that the court granted her full time to relieve her feelings, and every heart sympathized with the double and distressed orphan. I will not detail her entire testimony, but the part most interesting and damning in the case. She said, on the day of the murder her uncle and herself went to Frederick City, and in the afternoon she and her aunt were in Mr. Fisher's jewelry store looking at some jewelry, when her uncle passed by. They called him in, and her aunt begged him to buy a breast pin for her (Susan). He refused alleging that he had just paid his taxes and had spent all his money, and seemed angry at the increase of taxes over the year before, asserting that the farmers could scarcely pay them from the proceeds of the farm, and hurried them up to get ready to return home, as it was Saturday, and many things were to be done preparatory to the Sabbath. He requested them to remain there, and he would bring the carriage, and they would start home from there. They started, and on the way home she and aunt plagued uncle about the pin, jesting him about the people feeling so poor, and kept up a running conversation about people getting avaricious as they grew older, and he (uncle) evidently showed sorrow for not having purchased the pin. 'It was the first request he ever refused me, and showed regret at his petulance. Immediately after reaching home, he went up stairs for some tools, and brought down a remnant of a vest. It was made of a very thin, changeable silk, and was worn out around the pockets and collar. He called it his new vest, and said he would wear it to church the next day. She or aunt told him it was too much worn, and bantered him to bet them the breast pin mentioned, that they would so mend the rents and repair it as that he would not wear it to church with his coat unbuttoned. He accepted the bet, and went out. After supper aunt got down a bag containing scraps and pieces, and she and I cut out the frayed part of the vest, and together patched it with a piece of blood-red flannel. Uncle's bed was in the sitting room, and before we had completed the vest and made it as ridiculous as possible, he, as was his custom, went to bed. After completing the vest, we hung it on the bedpost, so he would see it the first thing in the morning, and we both believed he would not wear it.'

"At this point a vest found in young Markley's bundle when arrested was handed to her, and before unrolling it, she described the manner in which the patches were cut, and with what kind of dark and coarse thread they were inserted. She was nearly overcome when she unrolled the vest, and here, as described, was the identical vest, patched as she had described. It was the vest she had hung on the bedpost, and then came a crowd of associations too great for the poor heart-broken girl. She sobbed aloud and every eye in the court house but the prisoner's and neighbor P——'s were bedewed with tears. It was in proof that it was found in a small bundle of clothes in the possession of Markley when he was arrested. This, with his having been seen near the house two days before,—his many repeated threats,—his knowledge of the house, &c., confirmed the opinions of all that he was the guilty one. In answer to his attorney where he got the vest, he could say, 'he did not know.' To have carried a vest worth five cents and for three years and hundreds of miles, and never to have worn it, (nor could be—it was too large,) was alleged by all as special directions by Providence, leading to his conviction and punishment for the crime of murder most foul.

"Susan was recalled—'Where were you during the remainder of the night that you escaped the fire?' She answered: 'After placing the vest on the bedpost, I assisted aunt to do some mending, and after we had finished every thing, sitting by the fire, talking and laughing over uncle's surprise, when he would see the vest in the morning, we heard a rapping at the front door, and went with the candle to see who were there. We found a son and daughter of our next neighbor, Mr. P——, who had come over to get me to stay with them. They said their father sent them, as he had just heard that his father (living some ten miles distant) was taken suddenly ill, and he must go down and see him, and requested them to have me go over and stay with them during the night. I had often done so, and throwing on a bonnet and shawl, went with them. During the night we were awakened by old Mr. P——, who had returned, as he said, from his father's, and saw then the house on fire—hurried over, but never saw any one of the family alive. Several men were there, but so thoroughly on fire was the house that none of us dared venture within it.'

"The testimony of the coroner, and the party arresting young Markley closed the case, and resulted as I have already said,— and Markley was executed; denied any knowledge of the murder—but confessed seeing the house on fire, and leaving the country because of the house being burnt fearing he might be accused of it, and solemnly asserting that he never knew a murder had been committed, or that the house had been set on fire until after his arrest. He admitted that he had been in the neighborhood several days; had slept around on hay lofts, and was anxious to return to uncle's, but feared to do so; had a little money and got some slaves to purchase him whiskey and spent his time in the negro quarters, afraid or ashamed to return to his uncle's. He often hoped he could meet some of the family, either his aunt or Susan, and feared his uncle. All he regretted was that he did not go to his uncle and stay with him. He went to Baltimore, and seeing the house on fire, traveled by nights only; got aboard a coasting vessel, went south as a fisherman, and that was all he knew about it till his arrest.

"Before his execution he became very fat—and up to the last moment denied knowing anything of the murder or arson— seemed sorry for his uncle's and aunt's death—acknowledged he had made threats—confessed to having stolen the money for which he was convicted and arrested; he had no ill feelings against the members of the family, and dearly loved the children. He could easily be brought to tears when spoken to about the horrible tragedy, and manifested but little fear or anxiety about the future. The general impression was he would confess under the gallows, and that he was a hardened criminal indifferent to his fate—but at the last, when he saw no hopes of pardon, would confess the entire crime, and not till he saw no means of escape would he confess. All were disappointed, and to this moment, thousands regarded him as the most debased hardened wretch known to crime. The clergyman who visited him urged in the strongest terms to make his full confession, and was pained after each visit to report no progress in his moral condition. He heard but the same statements; could not break the thread of the denial, could not embarrass him by questions and felt fully convinced the poor miserable creature died with a 'lie in his mouth.' This accounts for his fre-

A DEATHBED CONVERSATION.

quent return to the trap door immediate before the execution. I doubt not he felt more anguish and sorrow than poor Markley, and on his knees he could but pray for forgiveness of the guilt, yet could not but be satisfied to reach the recess of the soul of the dying man, and believed, with all the denials of the guilt, that Markley added both impudent lies to a crime without parallel in the history of that State. He was a Christian and knew the power of confession and contrition. He could make no promise to one who would not confess—who showed no contrition—for there is none for such. He could only say, 'God be merciful to him a sinner,' without any assurance that his prayer could be heard or would be answered. He hoped on until the last moment, and left him with his God, without one assurance of future bliss or one hope of pardon. He knew if he could but open the secret recesses of his guilty heart, could but melt down his stubborn soul, could but get him to feel that he had committed a crime against humanity and the Supreme Being, that there were promises for even Markley, with the blood of seven souls upon his skirts; but to hear his denial, and, in most dogged terms, assert his innocence, his defiance of law, and more, the injustice of his punishment, was more than he could bear, and parted with him as one for whom in God's infinite mercy there is no place; nothing but 'wrath and a looking forward to a fiery and just indignation.' This occurred in 1830 [*sic*]. More than a quarter of a century after the writer met, in Washington City, a resident of Maryland he had not seen for 20 years. He is a physician and surgeon of most excellent reputation. His rides are extensive, and although he does not reside in Frederick county, has much surgical practice there. On retiring to bed after a pleasant afternoon with my friend we were compelled, from the crowd, (being at the house of a mutual friend) to sleep together, and I 'asked him how long it had been since the same thing had occurred.' We reckoned up the time and found it was at the period of the execution of Markley. When this time was judged the period, he spoke hurriedly and said, 'Do you know that poor fellow was innocent?' The question brought me from my bed, and there in the stillness of our room, 'the doctor' detailed the following facts:

"'I shall never forget that night. I sympathized with Markley on the gallows. I pitied him then, and never more fervently implored pardon for his horrible crime, but when I heard and was convinced that he was innocent, every sentiment of sorrow I ever conceived crowded upon me, and I resolved if by detailing these facts some other poor outcast could be spared from a punishment he did not merit, I would do a duty to my fellow man. This is my motive, and if my friend the doctor, should peruse these pages, he will forgive the publication by one who feels a duty he cannot avoid. Besides, a brother of Markley is buried in my town. He died without knowing the fate of an elder brother, but for the sake of one who faithfully performed his duty, although a maniac, these lines are written.

THE DOCTOR'S STATEMENT.

"I was sent for to see the Mr. P., mentioned in the preceding narrative, in consultation with Dr. J., of Frederick City. After

learning the history of the case, I expressed regret that I should
have been called so great a distance without any prospect of doing any good. He was excessively emaciated, was hypocondri-
acal [*sic*], and for weeks refused food. His physicians and family
had urged every argument to induce him to eat; had on many occasions forced him from his bed into a carriage; had, indeed, kept
him traveling for several weeks; had brought to bear upon him all
moral influence to break in upon his morbid fancies and supposed
imaginative sufferings, to no avail. The diagnosis was softening
of the brain; prognosis, death. He had been frankly informed but
the day before I saw him of these opinions, and thus was induced
to request my advice. I heard with interest all the statements
made by his son and daughter, as well as the physicians, and,
without arrogating to myself any special credit, I could not bring
my mind to their conclusions. Here was a man who lived in a
section of country proverbial for health and longevity; his mind
had never been overtaxed; his pursuits had been farming, and as
far as I know, or could ascertain, nothing ever in his long life had
greatly excited him. The loss of his wife did not greatly depress
him. He was prosperous; his eldest daughter remained to cheer
and comfort him, and his eldest son, with his family, occupied
the homestead, and the relations of the family had been, and
were then, most pleasant. He could not sleep without powerful
anodynes. Without knowing why, and you know it has frequently happened you in your practice, I conceived the idea there was
more in the case than physical suffering or physical change, and
my questions to him were pointed and searching, so much so
that I found I was on the right track, and he seemed conscious
of my possessing power over him. I told him frankly I was not
satisfied with all the statements made, but believed there were
other and deeper causes of his suffering. He said, pointing to his
heart, that it was there. I said, it may be there, but it is not in the
organ itself; it is in the emotions and feelings and acts that are
supposed by some physicians to be traced to the heart; and so believing, I knew he had not treated his family and physicians fairly in withholding from them anything that could throw light on
his singular affliction, and with emphasis said, you must confide
in me and tell me all. He asked me the duties of physicians as re-
cipients of secrets, and I repeated that noble oath of Hippocrates,
and said to him all properly educated men in the profession re-

garded it with sacredness, that it could not be trespassed upon by courts, kings or princes; and in his case I should be governed by its obligations. This was all he wanted, and requesting the room to be cleared and closed, he asked me to get pen and paper and write down what he was about to tell me. And promising his remarks particularly with the injunction of secrecy, during his life, and having received my promise that it should be obeyed in every particular, he commenced by asking me if I remembered the murder of the Markley [sic] family, and the execution of the nephew for the murder? I told him I did, most vividly. With much feeling, he then said: I committed that murder, and Markley was innocent. Now, doctor, write down what I tell you, and after I am dead, if you think it right, and if the feelings and interests of others will justify it, I desire its publication. I heard young Markley was in the neighborhood, skulking about barns and negro quarters, and I sought him. I invited him to come to my house, or rather to sleep in my barn, and furnished him with food and whisky for two days before the murder. On Saturday evening, I told my family I had heard of my father's illness, and that I would ride down to see him. I had often done so. I requested my son and daughter to go over to Markley's and get Susan to come over and spend the night with them. This, also, was usual. I waited until I saw them reach my house, and going to Markley's, got his axe, went to his room, and with one blow dispatched him, and with a second, his wife. With the same axe, I killed the three children, and whilst debating how to proceed in regard to the two old people, who slept up stairs, I heard a step on the stairs, and there encountered the old man, slew him, then walked up stairs and killed the old lady. I then set to work to fire the house in several places; did so, and as I was about to leave, saw the vest on the foot of the bed, mentioned by Susan rolled it up, put it in my pocket, and rode home. I awaited the full blaze of the house before I awoke young Markley, who was sleeping in my barn, and, without his seeing me, slipped the vest into his bundle, gave him three dollars, and told him to fly for his life, as he there saw the house burning, and he would be accused of the at, as he was in the neighborhood. He was very much alarmed, but after leaving me he said he would never be taken alive, as he would rather die than go again to the penitentiary. He told the truth; he did not then know that a murder had been committed, nor that he house had been set on fire. If accidental, he only feared he might be accused of the fire. I did not arouse my own family and Susan until I found the house so fully in flames as to be impossible for any one to enter. My only motive was revenge for Markley's beating me in the suit, and love for Susan, who, I hoped, would marry me when she had no home; and moreover, I believed I should have prospered in my suit to Susan, had not the Markleys [*sic*] objected. This, doctor, is my disease, and you cannot cure it. I could not die without a confession. I have fasted longer and remained longer without sleep than any living man, and this was the cause. Never for one hour at a time since has this scene been absent from my mind, waking or sleeping—along or in company, it is all the same. For myself, I ask no respect or sympathy; and if you, after consulting my relations, think best to publish this confession, you have my consent. I will take no prescription from you, and I hope I may be near the end of a life more miserable than I can describe or you think.' The doctor closed, and afterward I asked the result. 'He died that night.' 'Did you publish the facts?' 'I did not; but have the manuscript; read it to his relatives, and for their sake did not publish it.' 'Is it known or talked of in the neighborhood?' 'It was for a time, but not having the full facts and so long a time having elapsed, but little curiosity was excited; besides, the vest in Markley's possession, so fixed his guilt, that no man, unless he knew how it got there, but believes that a poor, miserable, worthless vest, was the means Providence used to bring to punishment a hardened, blackened villain.' "

"To THE PUBLIC.—Two men have, within one year, been executed in Ohio upon circumstantial testimony, and each, under the gallows, denied the murders for which they suffered. Samuel Covert, for the murder of the Roosa family, in Deerfield, Warren county, was executed last summer upon circumstantial testimony—I may detail the facts in a subsequent paper—and a month since W. H. Smith was hanged in Washington, Fayette county, denying the murder of Cook to the last moment. I will also review this case. One thing rest assured of, in either case was there anything so strong, so damning, as the threats of Markley and the possession of the vest. The loss of a thumb, in Covert's case, hung him—as the murderer's hand was bloody, and left the imprint on a window sill in escaping. Six victims in the Roosa family, seven in the Markley—a vest in one case, the loss of a thumb in the other—hung both men. One is now known to be innocent, and Samuel Covert died asserting that the 'guilty man would be known.' Covert's and Markley's characters hung them. They were bad men—but are all bad men hung?

"MEDICUS."[28]

The remains of the Newey massacre victims were buried in a spot commonly referred to as "the Newey graveyard," located near the place where the Appalachian Trail crosses Ritchie road in Washington county, Maryland. The Newey house was never rebuilt, and its dependencies were allowed to collapse. Today there is hardly a tangible reminder that the Neweys and their fellow victims ever existed. Yet regardless of who killed them, their horrible murders have immortalized them in local history. And notwithstanding the truth or falsity of Medicus's "strange story," people will debate the justness of Markley's fate as long as a shred of doubt exists.

---

[28] *The Carthage Weekly Banner* (Carthage, Mo.), March 30, 1867, p. 1.

VI.
Lewis the Robber—Part I.

TODD ANDREW DORSETT.

June 11, 2013.

Twenty-eight persons attended the sixth meeting of the Potomac Street Irregulars, held at the Parlor House. The evening's topic, David Lewis, has intrigued residents of central Pennsylvania and beyond for nearly two centuries. Moderator Dorsett focused on the traditions abounding about the magnanimity of this "Robin Hood of Pennsylvania," and thus left the subject open for further discussion at a later meeting. Accordingly, PSI Gary F. Johnson has since adopted Lewis's case, and will soon revisit it with the Irregulars in more depth.

IT is difficult, at this distant time, to differentiate between the facts pertaining to the life of David Lewis the counterfeiter and highwayman and the myth attaching to his many exploits. After perusing official records, contemporary newspapers, memoirs, and the pamphlet purporting to be Lewis's "confession," one can at least conclude that David Lewis was an adroit, attractive, engaging, and magnanimous individual who never shed blood or took human life. At the same time, the cynics amongst us will not hesitate to remind us that he was a crafty felon who kept the people travelling through central Pennsylvania in a constant state of anxiety; who abandoned two wives and at least two offspring, and who did on at least two occasions level his pistol at his adversaries and pull the trigger. Who, then, was David Lewis, the robber? And why should the Potomac Street Irregulars study him?

In his day, Lewis was the most celebrated criminal operating in Pennsylvania. Unfortunately, the haphazard manner in which the Commonwealth of Pennsylvania kept records for many years, together with infusions of partisan falsehood, has left a very muddled record of Lewis's career. For each person who claims that David Lewis was illiterate, there are several who insist he was an effective, gentlemanly schoolteacher. If one of his contemporaries would lambast Governor William Findlay for pardoning Lewis in his early days, thus prolonging his criminal career, surely there were members of Findlay's party who would rush to his defense. Similarly, there are various and contradictory assertions about Lewis's place of birth, socioeconomic status of his parents, his father's name, the reasons impelling Lewis into a life of crime, the circumstances surrounding his marriages (if in fact he was ever married), the specifics of his crimes and adventures, and even whether he made a confession during his final incarceration. Consequently, to answer "Who, then, was David Lewis, the robber?" with perfect specificity is virtually impossible.

To determine why this group should study Lewis is easier, although even that issue may excite some differences of opinion. Lewis is the perfect example of a lovable wrongdoer, and his case perfectly supports the enlightened position that no one makes a conscious decision "to be bad." Even writers who have not been kindly disposed towards Lewis have admitted he was generous towards the poor. Simultaneously, however, as all students of his life must acknowledge, Lewis was the terror of the well-heeled stranger who happened his way. Furthermore, it is generally accepted that he was possessed of so many talents that he should easily have been able to prosper without engaging in criminal activity. What, then, caused him to tread the wider path?

Like so many persons who turn to crime, David Lewis was bereft of his father at an early age. Afterwards, his widowed mother and her children struggled for their livelihood, and the mother eventually remarried twice. "Davy," the youngest of the Lewis children, is supposed to have left his home at age seventeen, and after two military enlistments in which he got into trouble (and honed his skills at getting *out* of trouble), he embarked on the career which has gained him immortality.

According to the purported, but certainly inauthentic, "confession" of David Lewis, he was born at Carlisle, Cumberland county, Pennsylvania, on March 4, 1790. When David was three years of age, his family removed to the vicinity of the present Milesburg, Northumberland (now Centre) county, his father having been appointed Deputy District Surveyor; but his father's death several years later left his family in straitened circumstances.[1]

After David Lewis left his mother's hearth, he was "employed in several occupations" before joining a "recruiting party" at Bellefonte, Centre county.[2] When the company sergeant pressed the matter of some petty infraction by Lewis, the latter decamped. After several months, Lewis enlisted as a private in Captain William N. Irvine's company of light artillery, and was accordingly mustered in, supposedly under the fictitious name of "Armstrong Lewis." After finding this situation too confining, Lewis deserted. His attempt to obtain a legal separation from that service was unsuccessful, and it also brought to light his desertion from his previous enrolment. The "confession" alleges that he was then court-martialed for desertion and double enlistment, found guilty, and sentenced to death.

Through the exertions of a number of persons, David Lewis's sentence was commuted to imprisonment. He was placed in confinement and shackled with various irons including a chain with a cannon ball attached to one end. At this time, Lewis made his first recorded prison break by sawing through his iron fetters, ingratiating himself to several soldiers, and running from the camp when an opportunity for escape presented itself. Supposedly this is also when Lewis selected "Lewis's cave" at Doubling Gap as his headquarters.[3] An early writer described this mountain fastness and its most famous inmate:

> "Part way up the knob, on the path to Flat Rock, are the remains of Lewis' Cave, a deep recess under a shelving rock. This was the retreat of Lewis, the robber, a notorious outlaw, well known throughout the counties adjoining this range of mountains. Here he hid from justice during the years 1816–20. Lewis practiced commu-

---

[1] C. D. Rishel, ed., *The Life and Adventures of David Lewis, the Robber and Counterfeiter: The Terror of the Cumberland Valley* (Newville, Pa.: C. D. Rishel, 1890), pp 34*ff. See also* "Central Pennsylvania's Robin Hood," *Harrisburg Telegraph* (Harrisburg, Pa.), November 26, 1938, p. 17. The Lewises probably dwelt in that part of Centre county which had been erected from part of Northumberland.

[2] This may be the period during which certain well-respected citizens remembered having David Lewis as a schoolmaster.

[3] Rishel at 35-38.

nism—at least he boasted that he was not a robber, but an equalizer, because he took from the rich and gave to the poor, single handed, usually, but sometimes with an assistant. He had fast friends in the few inhabitants of the gap, who would frequently assemble with him at the summer hotel, as then kept, and pass a jolly night at the expense of the generous outlaw."[4]

One writer, after visiting Lewis's cave, submitted a story about the bandit to a Washington newspaper. He noted that, although Lewis was an accomplished criminal,—

"yet he possessed traits of character which, as they stood out isolated, were noble even in depravity. He was reputed to be the handsomest and most perfectly formed man that had been seen—tall, majestic, possessing strength and agility unequalled. In single combat none could withstand his physical powers. Having been a small boy myself at the time of his career, a resident, too, of the neighbourhood, I well remember the fearful stories of his exploits, and can attest to his handsome, manly appearance from once accidentally seeing him as he passed by the home of my boyhood. He measured full 24 inches across the shoulders, was over six feet in height, and altogether of full proportions, yet his hands and feet so small and delicate that the securest irons or shackles could be slipped over them.[5] Owing to this peculiarity, he so often escaped from prison. It is said of him that he never committed murder, nor allowed it to be done by his companions.

"On one occasion, after perpetrating robbery, his friend Connelly proposed to kill the victim, alleging that 'dead men tell no tales.' Lewis remonstrated, and Connelly persisted. Finally, when the bloody deed was about being consummated, Lewis seized his rifle, commanding Connelly to desist, or his life should instantly pay the forfeit. He did so coweringly, and the man escaped with thankfulness, minus only filthy luchre."[6]

It is interesting to note the contradiction between the stories of Lewis's kindness and the newspaper items which cast him as

---

[4] S. D. Mowery in Rishel at 19.

[5] An account of Lewis's escape from the Chambersburg jail tends to contradict this assertion about Lewis's small extremities, for a posse searching for him found his shackles *cut off* in a wood near Chambersburg. "David Lewis—*Again*," *Republican Compiler* (Gettysburg, Pa.), June 7, 1820, p. 2, col. 1.

[6] "The Robber's Cave: Lewis, the Notorious Robber," *The Evening Star* (Washington, D. C.), September 2, 1854, p. 1, col. 6. *See also Republic Compiler*, October 20, 1819, p. 3.

a "dangerous man" without mentioning his redeeming qualities.[7]

After escaping from his military prison, David Lewis fled Pennsylvania in company with a Vermont peddler who initiated him into a band of counterfeiters. Not surprisingly, Lewis was good at his new craft, which he supposedly plied throughout New England and in parts of Canada and New York. He gradually made his way to New York City, where Mrs. John Jacob Astor was reputedly one of his victims. He met his first wife at Albany, New York, and abandoned her, probably at Philadelphia. Left with two small, motherless daughters, David remarried, to an amiable woman who reared his children. Despite professions of love, Lewis left both wives for the wild life of a highwayman in rural Pennsylvania.

During the last four years of his life, David Lewis frequented the hotel at Doubling Gap, then kept by one of his friends and supporters, one Howard. Tradition has it that when "the coast was clear" for Lewis to approach the hotel for refreshment and entertainment, Howard would hang a flag from the building's uppermost storey. When adverse parties were skulking about, then the robber would keep to his comfortably appointed cave under a rock shelf between the hotel and Flat Rock atop the nearby Round Knob. In these times of rustic seclusion, Lewis's friends (who appear to have been numerous in the nearby precincts), particularly one Robert Moffitt, catered to his needs.[8]

Local history is replete with accounts of David Lewis's chivalry, daring, and wit. Whether these tales are true is lost to modern scholars, but the stories are nevertheless interesting in our quest to understand the "Robin Hood of Pennsylvania." One of these first appeared in 1853 and was later reproduced in an eloquently written booklet published by one whose stated purpose was to counter the approbation which Lewis had gained because of his generosity and in spite of his treachery:

> "An old gentleman of Cumberland, Maryland, named Black, some years since related to the writer of this an adventure which he, from

---

[7] *See* "David Lewis—*Again*," *supra*; *Newbern Sentinel* (New Bern, N. C.), November 27, 1819, p. 3..

[8] Rishel at 19-20.

his own account, had with Lewis in the Allegheny Mountains. According to his story, he had crossed the mountains from Cumberland to (I think) Brownsville on horseback, for money. He rode a black horse, a fast runner, and while at Brownsville was bantered for a race. This was accepted, and the wager was one horse for the other. 'Blackey,' as he called him, won; and after Mr. B. received the money which was the object of his visit, he left the place with his prize, and staid that night at a friend's about six miles distant on his road home. In the morning his friend gave him a flask of excellent peach brandy which he pocketed, and then started for the mountains, riding the horse he had won, with 'Blackey' trotting after him. When he got into a lonely ravine, deeply shaded, a man sprang from over a high bank and in one or two bounds was on Blackey's back. The stranger immediately rode up along side, when Mr. B. distinctly perceived the outlines of a pistol in each pocket of his pantaloons. As might be supposed our informant felt something creeping over him like fear, but he attempted to conceal it. The stranger, riding peaceably along, commenced a conversation by remarking that 'he had seen "Blackey's" performance the day before, in the race, and was anxious to buy him.' Mr. B. remarked that he did not wish to sell the horse, as he had owned him for some time and would be sorry to part with him. His companion still appeared anxious to make the purchase, and Mr. B. having strong suspicions of his customer's real character, excited by the pistols and his unceremonious introduction, wished to get on the best possible terms with him. He therefore stopped at a spring on the road, and invited his companion to take some of the brandy. Several drinks were taken, he drinking cautiously, and his companion quite freely, from the mouth of

the flask. They again mounted and traveled without anything unusual happening, refreshing themselves several times from the flask. By and by they came to another spring, his companion by this time feeling sensibly the exhilarating effects of the brandy, and evidently in a very good humor. The conversation turned somehow on the loneliness of the mountains, the danger of robbers, &c., when his companion swore that he was not afraid of such characters, and pulled out his pistols to show that he was armed. He then asked Mr. B. if he had ever heard of Lewis, about whom there was so much ex-

citement, and for whose apprehension there were a number of rewards offered. Mr. B., putting the best face on the matter he could,
replied that he had not, and with a terrible stretch of conscience,
said he would like to see him; that he had heard a great deal about
him and about his bravery and magnanimity, etc. 'Would you like
to meet him in the mountains ? ' asked his companion. 'No,' said
Mr. B., 'I don't know that I would fancy that, but if I should, I do
not think I would stand in any danger of my life.' 'You would really
like to see him then ? ' again asked his companion, by this time pretty well intoxicated. 'Yes,' said Mr. B., quaking with fear, 'I would.'
'Well, sir,' replied the stranger, jumping to his feet, and bracing himself into an erect posture, 'here is Lewis—I am the man ! '

"'After getting over my affected surprise, and after some further
conversation,' said Mr. B., 'he declared that he had met me with the
intention of taking my money; that he knew how much I had, and
where I got it; but that I had treated him like a gentleman, and he
would not for the world harm a hair of my head, or take a cent from
my pocket.' Shortly after Mr. B. left without interruption, and the
last he saw of Lewis, as he turned a bend in the road, he was still
standing at the spring. Mr. B. remarked that he went along at a
careless and moderate pace until he got entirely out of sight of the
robber, but immediately after, the spirit and the flesh both moved
him to go as rapidly as the horses could travel.

"I have told the story as ' 'twas told to me,' and all I can say about
it is, that the gentleman who related it bore a highly respectable
character in Cumberland. What has become of him since, I know
not."[9]

Another legend relates that an Adams county posse pursuing
Lewis met a stranger. He inquired of their purpose, made further
inquiry about the outlaw Lewis, and then joined them for part of
their ride. During this time, he obtained some of their names and
addresses, and later sent them word "that they had been riding
for several hours in the company of Lewis, and he was anxious to
know whether they found his company agreeable."[10]

On another occasion, robber Lewis rode along the Walnut Bottom road with a gentleman, stopped him within sight of Centre-
ville, "and very politely made him deliver up his money. He then
took to the mountains and made his escape."[11]

---

[9] Rishel at 22-23.
[10] Rishel at 24.
[11] *Ibid.*

Perhaps the best illustration of Lewis's kindness and cunning is believed to have occurred in Mifflin county, Pennsylvania:

"Having failed of carrying into execution some of his deeply laid schemes for robbing several wealthy farmers during one of his marauding expeditions, and his finances getting uncomfortably low, he determined on making an effort to replenish at the first opportunity. Coming across a house that promised security from molestation, no other being near, he called at the door, and was admitted by an elderly female, of respectable appearance. Lewis, to ascertain where her money was kept, asked her to change a five dollar note. 'That unfortunately I am unable to do,' replied the woman, 'for I have not a dollar in the house; and, what is worse,' she added despondingly, as she caught a glimpse of a man coming through the woods some distance from the house, 'there comes the constable to take my cow for the last half-year's rent. I don't know what to do without her.' 'How much is due?' inquired Lewis, hurriedly. 'Twenty dollars, sir.' 'Have you no one to help you?' 'No one,' she replied. 'Then I will,' replied the robber as he drew from his pocket the exact sum, and threw it upon the table. 'Pay that fellow his demand, *and take his receipt*, but don't say anything about me.' Lewis had just time to make good his escape unobserved, when the worthy official arrived. He was proceeding without more ado to drive away the cow, when the woman came forward, paid him the money and took his receipt. He immediately set out on his return, but had not proceeded far, when Lewis bounded into the road and accosted him with 'How d'ye do, stranger? Got any spare change about you?' 'No!' simpered the frightened constable. 'Come, shell out old fellow or I'll save you the trouble,' returned Lewis as he presented a pistol at him. This argument convinced the constable that the fellow was up to his business, and he handed over his money as quickly as possible. Lewis got his own twenty dollars back, and forty dollars in addition. He often boasted that the loan of the twenty dollars was one of the best investments he had ever made."[12]

Once, in the mountains, Lewis stopped a man who was travelling from Pittsburgh to Philadelphia. After robbing the traveller, Lewis recognized him as a fellow who had helped him when he was in trouble. The bandit then restored the man's money to him and allowed him to resume his way unmolested.[13]

In early October 1819, Lewis and two others robbed a Pitts-

---

[12] Rishel at 24-25.
[13] Rishel at 25.

burgh merchant called McFarland as he passed through Bedford county. The highwaymen detained the man in the woods from nine o'clock in the morning until four o'clock in the afternoon, robbing him of fifteen hundred dollars. McFarland later reported that some of his captors wished to kill him, but that Lewis persuaded them to spare him. Soon an alarm was raised, and the robbers were apprehended and taken to Lewistown, and thence to the jail at Bedford. While being thus detained, Lewis managed to seize a pistol which had been carelessly left on a table near him, and he sprang to his escape but was forthwith recaptured. During this affray he reportedly snapped the pistol in his antagonists' faces twice, but the gun misfired both times.[14]

On April 19, 1820, Lewis and his frequent companion, one Connelly, a violent, desperate man, attempted to rob one Besore, a wealthy resident of southern Adams county. They failed, and Lewis was captured and lodged in the Carlisle jail. Once his oppressors realized that their captive was the celebrated Lewis, they transferred him to the jail recently erected at Chambersburg, which was considered the strongest prison in Pennsylvania.[15]

On May 25, 1820, David Lewis, in company with four others, escaped from the Franklin county stronghold.[16] Authorities offered a reward of three hundred dollars for his apprehension.[17]

On another occasion, Lewis, Connelly, and some colleagues had devised a scheme whereby they would divest Dr. Peter Shoenberger, an iron manufacturer of central Pennsylvania, of a great sum of money he was supposed to be collecting at the present Harper's Ferry, West Virginia. Dr. Shoenberger's plan was to return home by way of Baltimore and the road leading from that city to Pittsburgh. That itinerary would have taken him directly across the Antietam country of Franklin county.[18]

---

[14] "Daring Robbery," *Republican Compiler* (Gettysburg, Pa.), October 20, 1819, p. 3.

[15] *Republican Compiler*, May 3, 1820, p. 3.

[16] "David Lewis," *Republican Compiler*, May 31, 1820, p. 3.

[17] Broadside in possession of T. A. Dorsett, Waynesboro, Pa.

[18] David Lewis probably made numerous trips through the Antietam watershed, for he is known to have travelled from Fayette county, Pa., to Emmitsburg, Md., by the Maryland route. He also visited various parts of Franklin and Adams

Despite careful planning, the scheme to rob Dr. Shoenberger failed; for someone had warned the wealthy traveller of the bandits' designs, and he altered his course to elude Lewis and his conspirators. Lewis heard of this and likewise altered his plans. In the vicinity of Bellefonte, Centre county, the two parties met. After Lewis made his demand of Dr. Shoenberger, the latter, spying some teamsters on a nearby hill, called to them for help. At this, Lewis actually aimed his pistol at the doctor and pulled the trigger. Fortunately, his gun malfunctioned, but an angry Connelly approached the doctor with deadly intent. Only Lewis's remonstrance kept Connelly from killing their prey. Meantime, one of the teamsters shot Connelly who, with Lewis, escaped into a nearby wood.[19]

Yet another story supports the characterization of our redoubtable "Robin Hood" as a decent person:

"Long before this adventure of Doctor Shoenberger's, the old Keystone State was in a turmoil over the depredations committed by bands of brigands, who were guilty of the most heinous crimes. The inhabitants were in constant dread of the attacks of highwaymen. One of the most thoroughly organized of these was headed by Robber Lewis. It seems Robber Lewis did not deserve all the condemnatory reports in circulation about him. Many instances of kindness and a disposition to help the needy and distressed, by contributing to their wants, characterized his career. For these acts he never received any credit at the hands of his persecutors.

"In the month of October, 1815, a German named Jacob Simmons was crossing the mountains from Bellefonte to Lock Haven desiring to get on the direct road to Harrisburg. In those days travel was either on foot or by vehicles. Simmons was aware of the brigands that infested the country, yet he ventured to travel this mountainous region alone. He had hoarded up a few hundred dollars, and was going to Harrisburg to meet a brother who had just landed in this country, and both intended to travel westward to better their condition.

"Little did he think he would soon have the supreme pleasure of stopping with Robber Lewis and his colleagues. If he did he would not have taken his dangerous journey. He had accomplished scarcely half of the trip, when the sun began to sink out of sight. He had

---

counties, thus hardly being able to avoid passing through this region.
[19] Rishel at 26-27.

heard of the many depredations and robberies committed by Robber
Lewis and his daring companions, who were at that time invading
the country around about. Simmons began to feel uneasy. He felt
for the leather belt around his waist and, satisfied that his money
was safe, continued his lonesome journey. The gloom convinced
him that midnight darkness would soon overtake him, and he had
yet a dozen miles or more to travel. The German became almost
paralyzed with fear. Every sound he heard presented a horrifying
picture of highwaymen jumping out from behind some tree or rock
and demanding his money. He resolved to look for shelter and ask
for a night's lodging at the first house he would reach. He had traveled only a few hundred yards farther, when he discovered a cabin
in the wood by the side of the road. Upon investigation he found it
to be occupied, and knocked on the rude door. It was opened by a
man of fine personal appearance, who invited him in. In one corner
of the cabin was a rude hearth, built of stone, upon which blazed
a glowing fire. The cheerfulness of the interior acted like a magic
charm on him, and served to dispel all his fear. Robber Lewis and
his fearless band could now attack their victims. Simmons was all
right; at least he thought so.

"Sitting beside the blazing fire, which lit up the room, the German
felt safe enough. This was one of Robber Lewis' stopping places.
Besides himself there were three of his companions in the cabin.
They were all sitting around the fire enjoying a smoke with their
pipes, and Simmons was cordially invited to join them.

"The German unfolded himself and related his whole story to
them, where he had been working, how much money he had, and
whither he was going; that night had overtaken him, and he was
afraid of being robbed by highwaymen, and that he concluded not
to go any farther, and run the risk of losing his money. They listened
with interest to his narrative and assured him that he was perfectly
welcome, and that no harm would befall him while under their protection, for which Jacob thanked them very much.

"During the evening the conversation drifted to various subjects
and the stories circulated by the inhabitants of the surrounding
country, the German very often mentioning the name of Robber
Lewis and his desperate followers. He referred to the robberies
committed by the lawless bandits, who were a terror to that section
of the State, where they made their power felt. The remarks of the
German caused more than one smile to light up the countenances of
the robbers during the evening. Before the coterie retired Simmons
was given a bounteous supper by his host, and all sought rest, the
German feeling grateful for their taking him in and protecting him
from the dangers that threatened him should he have continued his
journey that night.

"When morning dawned the German descended a rude ladder to the room below. To his amazement he beheld a table loaded down with many of the luxuries of life. How fortunate he was ! He was invited to make a hearty breakfast, as he had many hours of travel before him. After he had completed his meal and regained his lost vitality, he started on his journey. Before taking his leave, he asked what he owed. 'Nothing, sir,' was the reply, 'but you can inform your friends that you stopped with Robber Lewis and his colleagues!'

"After Simmons had been informed by the robber chieftain that he could go on his way rejoicing, without any fear of being robbed, he could hardly express his feelings of gratitude for the kindness received at the hands of his benefactor, who had been painted in his mind as a murderer and a destroyer of innocent life. He was much surprised to find a different man than had been represented to him.

"Robber Lewis had many good traits, and was never known to have shed blood, or to have taken a human life. He invariably stole from those who could afford it and gave to the poor. His acts of charity will always be commemorable to those who remember him. This little instance of Jacob Simmons' is, no doubt, remembered by many of the residents of Pennsylvania."[20]

Lewis's attempt to rob Dr. Shoenberger caused an alarm to be raised in the neighbourhood. On July 2, 1820, a posse captured Lewis and Connelly during a gunfight near Driftwood, in Centre (now Cameron) county.[21] Connelly soon died from the wound he received in the affray, but Lewis was taken to Bellefonte, the county seat of Centre. During the capture, a gunshot had shattered one of his arms; he refused friends' urgings to have the limb amputated, and he died from gangrene in the jail at that place on July 13, 1820.

One announcement of David Lewis's death compared him to a great bandit in European literature:

"DAVID LEWIS—*no more.*

"BELLEFONTE, (Penn.) July 21.
"Died on Wednesday evening last, in the jail of this county, the noted David Lewis (the American Aballino) in the 30th year of his age.
"A jury of Inquest was held on his body, who found similar to the

---

[20] Rishel at 27-29.
[21] *See* "David Lewis," *Republican Compiler* (Gettysburg, Pa.), July 5, 1820, p. 5.

one held on the body of Connelly. For some time before his death he endeavoured by prayer and supplication to make peace with his God, and obtain forgiveness of his sins. He forgave those who were the instruments in the hands of the Almighty in arresting him in his wicked career. May his death be a warning to all those who are embarked in the same kind of business, and serve as a terror to evil doers."[22]

Shortly after David Lewis's death, someone published a pamphlet purporting to be his autobiography and confession. Those who waited upon him during his incarceration, including the sheriff, the jailer, and a clergyman, certified that Lewis made no such confession, but that he did make a brief, general statement "that he had been a bad man."[23]

The "confession," which has always been suspected of being a political pamphlet aimed at defeating Governor Findlay, includes this statement:

"If there was any class or description of people in society whom I would sooner have robbed than any other, it was those who held public offices, and under color of law had been guilty of extortion; who had plundered the poor, and cheated the widow and the orphan. Against such workers of iniquity my mind had taken a set, and I was determined never to spare them on any occasion that offered. The groans of the distressed, the cries of the widow, and the complainings of the oppressed rang in my ears, and called aloud for vengeance. There was perhaps no place in the State in which I heard more complaints of this sort than in the county of Cumberland, and as Carlisle was my native place, for which I felt a strong attachment, instead of committing a wrong I conceived that I would be rendering society a service by punishing those official marauders who infest the town, in visiting upon them the same degree of severity which they had visited upon others, and thus, 'make the cruet feel the pains they gave.'"[24]

The exploits of "Davy" Lewis throughout central Pennsylvania are ripe for study at some future meeting. Meanwhile, some

---

[22] "David Lewis—*no more,*" *The Maryland Gazette* (Annapolis, Md.), August 3, 1820, p. 2.

[23] "From the Bellefonte Patriot," *Republican Compiler*, October 4, 1820, p. 4

[24] Rishel at 66-67..

Pennsylvanians still believe that there is booty to be found where Lewis the Robber secreted it two centuries ago. The Robin Hood of Pennsylvania himself reposes at Milesburg, Centre county.

"Had Lewis' mind been directed into the right channel and subjected to a proper course of training, he might have lived an honor to himself and his family and been useful in his day and generation; but having a penchant for the romantic and lawless, where he could indulge his passions without restraint, he became alienated from society, an outcast and a byword, and in his death we have but another proof of the truthfulness of the proverb that 'the way of the transgressor is hard.'"[25]

---

[25] Raftsman's Journal (Clearfield, Pa.), March 26, 1856, p. 1, col. 1.

VII.
The Shockey Counterfeiting Ring.

JOHN MICHAEL LOGAN.

July 9, 2013.

Thirty-five persons attended the seventh meeting of the Potomac Street Irregulars, held at the Parlor House. PSI J. Michael Logan recounted the well-known story of the Eighteenth-century counterfeiting ring led by Valentine Shockey. PSI Darlene Shockey Weddle loaned a substantial part of the source material, and PSI Franklin Shockey guided PSI Logan to Shockey's Cave.

𝕿HE complete story of the network of counterfeiters and thieves who operated in the Middle Atlantic colonies during the War of Independence transcends the scope of this organization. Portions of it will nevertheless hold great interest for students of local history, for important aspects of the counterfeiting operations occurred on South Mountain and in the valley within its shadow. It involved one of the best-known families living along Mason and Dixon's line, and cost at least one member of that clan his life.

During the Revolution, the British Government knew well that one way to weaken the united American colonies was to devalue their currency. As a result, both the British and some Americans counterfeited Continental money. Sometimes the inauthentic British money, which was usually printed using engraved plates, was actually superior to the genuine Continental scrip, which was produced with set type. For enterprising Americans who had no scruples about enriching themselves at the expense of the war effort, this situation offered a fine opportunity; but in so doing they were committing a capital offense.

John Christopher Shockey was a German immigrant who on July 12, 1868, had located a plantation of eighteen hundred twenty acres called "Sarah's Delight" along the foot of South Mountain between the present villages of Ringgold, Maryland,

and Rouzerville, Pennsylvania. He and his wife had a large family, of whom these four are known to have been involved in the making or uttering of counterfeit Continental money: Valentine, Isaac, Abraham, and Christopher. The son of John Christopher from whom all the Shockeys now residing in the Antietam county descend—Jacob—was apparently never involved in his brothers' criminal activities. The youngest brother, Christopher, is the one who paid the supreme penalty for uttering some of the brothers' illegal product.

The State authorities were rigorous in their quest to vanquish these thieves. At a special meeting on February 2, 1777, the Committee of Observation for the Elizabeth-Town[1] district of Washington county, Maryland, brought before it one John Tedrow,[2] accused of uttering counterfeit Virginia money. The minutes of that meeting disclose the following:—

"John Tedrow, a Prisoner in this Town, for passing counterfeit Virginia Money, was brought before Committee, upon Examination confessed that he went to Isaac Shockeys on tuesday the 21st of Jany last tarried there some Days that s^d Shockey agreed to give him the s^d Tedrow 150 Dollars of s^d Counterfeit Money, in order to pass out of which Tedrow was to return one half, but that afterwards s^d Shockey only gave him 78 Dollars, saying there was no more sign'd, and that the person who sign'd the Money, would sign no more, at that time, because he purpos'd to have it press'd, thinking it not yet compleat, that said Tedrow when pass'd what he had receiv'd, was to repair to s^d Shockey for more, who promised to supply him therewith, and that he the s^d Tedrow might return what he pleas'd in Lieu of the 78 Dollars receiv'd that there was at Shockey's a certain Person dress'd in white Broad-Cloath Coat Jacket and Breeches, with a velvet Cape on Coat, whom he the s^d Tedrow suspected to be the Signer of s^d Money, that s^d Tedrow asked s^d Shockey that Gentleman's name, Shockey replied he knew it not, and that he refus'd to tell his Name to any person, that a certain Christian Hearn was at Shockeys in Company with the aforesaid Gentleman, said he was a Captain, and came on purpose to Recruit.

his

Sign'd John   X   Tedrow

Mark

---

[1] Now Hagerstown.

[2] Probably John *Detrow*, or *Dutterow*, whom Mark Milligan later accused of complicity with the Shockey counterfeiters.

"Upon receiving the aforegoing Confession of John Tedrow it is ordered that a strong Guard be sent to apprehend Isaac Stophel, Felty and Abraham Shockey, and all others whom they may have reason to suspect to be concern'd with the said Counterfeit Virginia money and them or either of them bring before this Committee to answer s[d] Charge and likewise to bring all Counterfeit money, Materials thereto belonging, and all fire Arms that may be found in their or either of their possessions."[3]

The Committee of Observation met again the next day and reported that the guard sent to apprehend the Shockey brothers had indeed delivered to them "the Bodies of Isaac, and Christian Shockey, who on Examination denied the Charge of being privy to, or concern'd with the making and passing Counterfeit Virginia Money." They ordered that the alleged counterfeiters "be confin'd in Irons in the Common Goal for this County untill legally discharged therefrom. Recd from the Guard a Rifle Gun got at Valentine Shockey's marck'd on the Butt W. S."[4]

On February 4, at another special session, one John Acton was brought before the Committee of Observation, "charg'd with writing & sending a Letter to Isaac Shockey at said Shockey's Request, to the Intent that said Shockey and his Banditti might rescue John Tedrow a Prisoner, (for passing Counterfeit Virginia Money) from the Guard who then had said Tedrow in Custody, upon Examination acknowledged the Charge." The committee ordered that Acton be kept in irons, closely confined in the "common Goal" until legally discharged.[5]

In his centennial history of Waynesboro, Benjamin Matthias Nead described the capture of one of the Shockey brothers:

"Well known through all this section of country through the period of the revolution and down to later days was the notorious band of counterfeiters, highwaymen and horse thieves, who carried on their depredations through the territory extending from the borders of Virginia through all parts of the Cumberland, Lancaster and Chester valleys. Chief among these desperadoes were the Nugents,

[3] *Maryland Historical Magazine*, Vol. XIII (Baltimore: The Maryland Historical Society, 1918), pp. 229-230.

[4] *Ibid.* at 231.

[5] *Ibid.*

the Doanes and the Fritzes, and so extensive was their business as to furnish constant employment for many agents all along the route and even into Canada. It is not possible here to tell in detail the romantic history of these notorious characters, but mention has already been made by others of some of their operations in the South mountain. A local write entertainingly tells, in a chapter of 'Unwritten Local History,' published some time ago in a Waynesboro paper, of the doings of some of the confederates of this gang.

"It was the province of the brave settler to defend himself against every character of attack, and so it is that when the presence of these members of the gang whom the writer calls 'the two brothers, Shockke,' was suspected in the South mountain, an attacking party under the lead of Colonel James Johnston and 'Squire' John Bourns was formed, and the mountain scoured in search of the marauders. The colonel, with a squad of his daring troops, accompanied by 'Squire' Bourns, marched into the mountain, and thus entertainingly their exploit is recounted:

"'A brief halt was made, then the march, or rather dash, was resumed, and up and into the mountains they rode, accompanied by citizens, until they had approached so near the hiding resort that absolute quiet became needful in every movement. Strategy had been planned, the countersign given out, and, dismounted, the party divided, walking stealthily apart through the dense woods to surround the marauders' den or cave.

"''Squire Bourns appeared rather as a non-combatant; he simply had a staff in his hand. Bur for the night's darkness he might have been noticed, however, to wear at his side a bayonet, as he wore that weapon when a soldier under Washington three years before.

"'The night waned, and the silence continued through the forest, interrupted only by the occasional bark of a fox, or the hoot of an owl. But as the morning began to dawn the soldier's intent ear caught from a little distance a rustling sound like that made by animals moving through the underbrush; and quickly its cause was revealed in the approach of a man whom Bourns in the twilight mistook to be one of his party who wore a military hat; and by the planned whistle he called for the countersign. This was not returned, and, being in doubt, the canny Scot started toward the man whom he followed until the growing light proved the fugitive was bent on eluding him; and he immediately shouted the battle rally for his party to hear and join him. Being fleet afoot, 'Squire Bourns gained on the disguised marauder, who proved to be one of the brothers, Shockke, and he ordered him to halt and surrender. The man, without halting, looked back, muttering an angry reply; and making a misstep he fell to the ground, when the "Squire," coming up, had his bayonet instantly in use to keep his burly foe from rising. Within a very few minutes Colonel Johnston, with the rest of the loyal party, rode up; when the march was started upon down the mountains homeward, with the prisoner in company.'"[6]

The man caught on the aforementioned occasion was the younger Christopher Shockey, who became one of five men hanged in Pennsylvania between 1779 and 1782 for counterfeiting-related crimes against the commonweal.[7] He was, however, the only member of the Shockey family to forfeit his life for these crimes.

Christopher Shockey had served as a private in Colonel Thomas Hartley's Seventh Regiment of the Pennsylvania Line. Upon dissolution of the regiment in February 1779, Shockey returned to Franklin county. On April 23, same year, he visited several establishments at Carlisle, Pennsylvania, where he passed, or uttered, some counterfeit Continental money. Complaints made the next day by businessmen who had accepted Shockey's counterfeit money resulted in the search party described above.[8]

Denied bail, Christopher Shockey was lodged in the Cumberland county jail at Carlisle. On October 18, 1779, a grand jury found a true bill against him for knowingly counterfeiting and uttering thirty-four pieces of counterfeit Continental thirty-dollar bills. Trial in the case commenced on October 20. Shockey pleaded not guilty. A jury of twelve men acquitted him of counterfeiting but found him guilty of uttering false money. The court sentenced him to death by hanging.[9]

On November 23, 1779, after considering several petitions for leniency in behalf of Christopher Shockey, the Supreme Executive Council of the Commonwealth of Pennsylvania issued a warrant for Shockey's execution to occur on December 11. Shockey himself had submitted the following to the council:—

---

[6] Benjamin Matthias Nead, *Waynesboro: Centennial History, 1797–1900* (Harrisburg, Pa.: Harrisburg Publishing Company, 1900), pp. 112-114, quoting Dr. J. Francis Bourns in "Unwritten Local History," *The Village Record* (Waynesboro, Pa.), September 1895.

[7] Henry J. Young, "Treason and its Punishment in Revolutionary Pennsylvania," *Pennsylvania Magazine of History and Biography*, July 1966, pp. 287*ff.*

[8] John Howard McClellan, "Colonial Counterfeiters of the Blue Ridge," n.p., 1989.

[9] *Ibid.*

*"The Petition of Christopher Shockey
now in the Jail in Carlisle*

"Most Humbly Sheweth: That your petitioner has been indicted and convicted for having passed counterfeit money and has received Judgment of Death.

"Your petitioner has been three years a soldier in Col. Hartley's Regiment in the Continental Service and during that period has fully discharged his duty as a solider and would continue to render his services in that way to his Country. But, his present deplorable situation prevents him and having a wife and three small children, he most earnestly solicits and prays for your Honour's clemency and mercy and that your Honours, in consideration of his past service and helpless family will grant him a pardon of his offense and of the awful penalty to which he is sentenced.

"And your petitioner will is as Duty bound pray,

CHRISTOPHER SHOCKEY

"Unhappy Brother in the Temple of Fame

"Carlisle Jail

"26 October, 1779"

These petitions were futile. Shockey and several others who had been sentenced to death were hanged at Carlisle on or about the appointed date.[10]

It is interesting to note that Christopher Shockey, who was hanged at Carlisle, had twice deserted from his army service not many months prior to the dissolution of his regiment and his return home. Whilst he admitted to deserting, he blamed his brother Abraham, also a member of the regiment, for inducing him to do so, and gave as his defense the fact that he had heard that his wife and three children had been put out of their residence. He claimed to have indeed found them, upon his de-

---

[10] *Ibid. See also Colonial Records of* Pennsylvania, Vol. XII (Harrisburg, Pa.: Theo. Fenn & Co., 1853), p. 179. *Cf. The Pennsylvania Packet* (Philadelphia, Pa.,), November 27, 1779, p. 3: "We hear that . . .execution of the sentence of death, lately pronounced at Carlisle, against Christopher Shockey, for the counterfeiting [*sic*] of paper money, Thomas Madden for highway robbery, and Thomas Story for murder, is ordered to be done at Carlisle, on Wednesday the 8th of December next."

sertion homeward, living in his brother's stable. When Christopher Shockey and one John King, Jr., were sentenced to death for desertion, the youthful King was considered worthy of a pardon, and Shockey of a hanging.[11]

Only two weeks after Christopher Shockey was sentenced to death, a close associate of the Shockey brothers—Christian Hoover—confessed to the same crime for which Shockey had been hanged; but Hoover claimed the benefit of clergy,[12] and he was merely branded with a "T" on his left thumb and sentenced to about one year's imprisonment.[13]

About the time Christopher Shockey was captured on the mountain and imprisoned at Carlisle, an important event in the prosecution of the counterfeiters occurred at York, Pennsylvania. Mark Milligan, of Black's Gap, Franklin county, was accused of possessing counterfeiting stamps, a misdemeanor. As if there were no honor among thieves, Milligan agreed to make a statement implicating a number of transgressors in return for leniency regarding his own punishment. Accordingly, Milligan appeared before David Jamison and William Scott, justices of the peace for York county, and gave the following deposition on September 10, 1779:

> ". . .about three years ago Isaac and Abraham Shockey and John Dutterow came to the examinant at his home in Black's Gap and said they knew he could engrave and requested him to engrave plates for them to counterfeit money; that he engraved plates of eight dollar bills and that John Dutterow paid this examinant thirty pounds for them. That said Dutterow lives sometimes at Shockey's and sometimes at his brother's about 20 miles from Shockey's in the State of Maryland.
>
> "That two years ago, this examinant was applied to by Joseph

---

[11] Edward G. Lengel, *ed.*, *The Papers of George Washington,* Revolutionary War Series, Vol. 15 (Charlottesville: University of Virginia Press, 2006), pp. 388-89.

[12] The Act of the legislature under which Shockey and Hoover were accused specifically excluded benefit of clergy as a means of avoiding the death penalty, yet Hoover pleaded successfully for it. Benefit of clergy allowed literate citizens one chance to avoid the death penalty by reading a specific scripture. If the defendant successfully read the scripture, then his death sentence was commuted.

[13] McClellan, *supra.*

Nicholson[14] of Nicholson's Gap, York County and John King, since a soldier, to engrave plates for them to counterfeit money. That he engraved a plate to strike five dollar bills and a plate to strike seven dollar bills, for which they paid near one hundred fifty pounds. * * *

"Sometime after, Valentine Shockey applied to him for two thirty dollar stamps for which he received fifty pounds apiece. (The Chief Justice has one of his notes from a plate for a large $8.) That afterwards he was taken up and admitted to bail by the Chief Justice; that he was applied to about the latter part of April by Abraham and Isaac Shockey to make prints of the forty dollar plates, now in the possession of Mr. Archibald McLean, but that he put them off, under some pretence and did not do it for them. That a family by the name of Cook, who live in Black Water, in the State of Virginia have a press and strike counterfeit money.

"That Valentine Shockey and Isaac Shockey applied to this examinant to go and sign money for the Cooks. That 'Felty' Shockey signs their own emissions and he saw the Shockeys strike their money different times. That they do it with an instrument like a lemon squeezer.

"That James Thompson of Conococheague, near to James Campbell's Tavern has a bill of Felty Shockey's making and signing. That Hugh Welsh, who served part of his time with Clerk near Black's Gap has a quantity of Shockey's money. * * *

"That all the Newgents are concerned with the Shockeys and pass their money. That one Roseburgh who lives in the Mountain is concerned with the Shockeys and passes their money," &c.[15]

Milligan's deposition laid the foundation for the ensuing war on the counterfeiters.

Abraham and Isaac Shockey both survived their counterfeiting careers in the Antietam country, and settled in western States where they later died, leaving descendants.

Of all the Shockey brothers, the eldest, Valentine, or "Felty," had the most astonishing career. He became the owner of that part of his father's sprawling acreage which later embraced the George Harbaugh farm (more recently the "Glen Afton" property of the late D. Eldred Rinehart) located along Harbaugh Church

---

[14] Probably one of the sons or grandsons of Edward *Nichols*, an early settler in what is now Washington township, Franklin county. His surname as well as the appellation of the mountain gap named for him are often stated as either "Nicholas" or "Nicholson."

[15] *Calendar of Maryland State Papers* (Red Books), p. 146, Maryland State Archives. *See Also* McClellan, *supra*.

road between Midvale and Edgemont. The residence of Valentine Shockey is said to have stood between the present limestone dwelling house[16] and the barn on that farm. Maryland historian John Thomas Scharf described Valentine as "a daring and desperate man, and the boldest of the counterfeiters who followed on the heels of the Revolution."[17]

The Shockeys used a cave on South Mountain as their headquarters. Located atop the outcropping of boulders on the hill immediately east of the road leading from Cascade, Maryland, to Buena Vista Springs, Pennsylvania, opposite the "Cascades," it would provide not only protection from intrusion but also a good view of the nearby countryside. Popularly known as "Shockey's Cave," or sometimes "Shockey's Office," the counterfeiter's den was dynamited shut during Prohibition in order to prevent moonshiners from using it for their own illegal operations.

The following account of an attempted capture of "Felty" probably describes what occurred in 1777 after the Committee of Observation ordered his arrest:

"Once, when a posse were in hot pursuit of the counterfeiter, they came to his house in the evening, but he escaped to the mountain. They waited for some time, and then set fire to this house, with the hope that the sight of the flames would lure him from his hiding-place, and if he should come to the rescue, they might be able to capture him. The flames soon enveloped the building, and on the woods around and from the distant mountain shone the red glare of the burning house. From the side of the mountain Shockey looked down on the work of destruction, but he did not leave his retreat."[18]

On June 16, 1780, C. J. McKean wrote to President Joseph Reed of

---

[16] Erected by George Harbaugh in 1805.
[17] J. Thomas Scharf, A.M., *History of Western Maryland* (Philadelphia: Louis H. Everts, 1882), Vol. I., p. 614.
[18] *Ibid.*

the Supreme Executive Council that one Daniel Zuber, who had
been convicted of counterfeiting or uttering, had fingered Valentine Shockey "as his Seducer." The letter described Shockey as
being "at the head of the Banditti in York county, who debase the
Continental Currency by counterfeits; as he lives on the Maryland Line, and is not only artful, but daring, we have not yet been
able to apprehend him."[19]

On September 10, 1780, the Cumberland county grand jury
found a true bill against one Benjamin Musselman, of Washington township, for larceny. When Musselman "came clean,"
he likewise accused Valentine Shockey of persuading him into
wrongdoing.[20]

Despite his cunning, Valentine Shockey was eventually apprehended, having been accused of using "pewter, lead and other
base metals" to make counterfeit coins in Franklin township,
York (now Adams) county.[21] But, March 5, 1787, he and two
other prisoners escaped from the York county jail. A total of
eighteen dollars reward was offered for their recapture. Valentine was described as "about 5 feet 3 or 4 inches high, stout built,
swarthy complexion, his eyes commonly are watering, had on
a brownish great coat lined with linsey, blue woolen stockings,
and a double breasted striped linsey jacket, a large wool hat."[22]

Valentine Shockey, apparently rearrested, nevertheless once
again avoided his fate, as this newspaper item attests:

> "At the assizes held at York-Town, for the county of York, from
> the 9th to the 14th inst. The following culprits were tried—Philip
> Nagle, sentenced to be hanged, for coining French crowns, quarter
> dollars, &c. William Robertson, sentenced to the wheelbarrow for
> 14 years—Mark Millengen, for 10 ditto—Wells, Stanlier and Cun-
> ningham, each for 5 years.—Jeffe Cox, for the murder of his uncle,
> and Valentine Shockey, for coining money were acquitted."[23]

On February 13, 1787, while incarcerated at York, Valentine

---

[19] Pennsylvania Archives, Vol. VIII (Philadelphia, Pa.: Joseph Severns & Co., 1853), p. 331.

[20] McClellan, *supra.*

[21] *Ibid.*

[22] *Carlisle Gazette*, March 1787.

[23] *The Pennsylvania Packet*, July 12, 1788, p. 2. Shockey's old colleague John Rosborough was likewise acquitted at that time.

Shockey sold his two hundred acres to Jacob Harbaugh, of Frederick county, Maryland, for the sum of one thousand pounds. On September 1, 1804, Harbaugh in turn conveyed the farm to his son George who built the present dwelling house. Following his acquittal, therefore, Valentine Shockey left Pennsylvania and settled in what was then Frederick county, Virginia. He dwelt in the vicinity of Berkeley Springs (now West Virginia) and continued his counterfeiting career as of old:

> "MARTINSBURGH (P. [*sic*]) Jan. 14.
>
> "MONEY MAKERS.—For some time past suspicions were entertained, that base money was made in the shop of a certain Streithoff near Sleepy Creek, in this County. To realize these suspicions and detect the persons engaged in this nefarious procedure, a party of persons surrounded the shop on Friday last.—The shop was found closed. On the party approached near the door when he distinctly heard the jingle of money. They demanded admittance—the demand was not complied with—the door was then forced open, when four men apparently much dismayed, were discovered; these men were Compsey, Dowson, Streithuff & the far-fame'd and well known Shockey. Many base dollars were found, together with a number of crucibles, a quantity of the necessary ingredients for preparing the metal, and all were then arrested and brought to Martinsburgh jail.
>
> "Their trial came on yesterday before a Court of inquiry in this town, when the Court, after examining the witnesses and hearing the pleadings, against and in favor of the prisoners, adjudged them to be sent to the District Courts holden at Winchester for further trial.[24]

On April 15, 1803, a Frederick county grand jury sitting at Winchester found true bills against all four men discovered at Streithoff's shop. They indicted them for felonious counterfeiting of United States silver dollars of the mint emission of 1795 through 1798. At a trial spanning the next two days, all but Dowson were convicted. Streithoff and Cumsey each received sentences of four years at hard labor or solitary confinement in the new penitentiary at Richmond.

Valentine Shockey received a harsher sentence: On May 23,

---

[24] *The Evening Post* (New York, N. Y.), January 29, 1803, p. 3.

1803, the court noted that "the said Shockey is a man of infamous character," and even though he had never been convicted previously, the court sentenced Valentine to a term of six years at hard labor or in solitary confinement in the penitentiary.[25]

Nothing further is known of Valentine Shockey. He was approximately sixty-one years of age when sentenced to hard labor or solitary confinement, and presumably died at Richmond after he had successfully eluded the wages of counterfeiting for thirty years.

In 1856, Dr. Henry Harbaugh, who was born on the old Valentine Shockey farm, wrote about the Shockey counterfeiters:—

> "The exploits of this terrible gang, of which [Valentine] Shockey was the leader, would make quite a chapter of wicked daring, if collected and recorded. Shockey's cave and its traditions will not soon pass from the memory of the generations in that region of country, and some Stilling may yet arise who will spin out the rough romantic history of Shockey, into the dimensions of 'Rinaldo Rhinaldinni.' We remember as a boy, to have turned up with the harrow in the plowed meadow, a zinc plate, the counterfeit type of a Continental note. * * *"[26]

---

[25] McClellan, *supra.*

[26] Rev. H. Harbaugh, *Annals of the Harbaugh Family in America, 1736–1856* (Chambersburg, Pa.: M. Kieffer & Co., 1856), pp. 70-71.

CONTINENTAL CURRENCY, 1776.

Counterfeit Continental Currency.

Early Twentieth-century postcard view of "Shockey's Cave."

SCHOCKEY'S CAVE NEAR BUENA VISTA, BLUE RIDGE MOUNTAINS, PA.

Site of Valentine Shockey farmstead, Harbaugh Church road. His dwelling house stood between the house and barn pictured. (Courtesy of Mrs. Darlene Shockey Weddle)

ABOVE: *Young people from the vicinity of Carlisle at Lewis's Cave, Doubling Gap, Pa., in the early Twentieth century.*

(Courtesy of Cumberland County Historical Society)

RIGHT: *Nineteenth-century artist's conception of David Lewis during his final confinement, at Bellefonte, Pa.*

LEWIS'CAVE-DOUBLING GAP PA.

David Lewis (1790–1820), *the "Robin Hood of Pennsylvania," often resorted to this cave at Doubling Gap, Cumberland county, Pa., when pursued by legal authorities. It is situated midway between the old Doubling Gap hotel and the summit of the mountain. Tradition insists that the hotelkeeper would hang a certain flag from the upper storey of his establishment to signal to "Davy" that the coast was clear for him to come partake of refreshment and entertainment.*

Numerous caves and buildings in central Pennsylvania gladly claim association with the legendary, charismatic bandit who might have prospered had his remarkable energy and talents been channelled into lawful activities.

(Courtesy of Cumberland County Historical Society)

FOLLOWING PAGE: 1820 *broadside proclaiming the rewards offered for the apprehension of David Lewis and other prisoners who had escaped with him from the Franklin County Jail at Chambersburg, Pa. Less than two years old at the time, the jail was considered the strongest prison in the Commonwealth.*

(Courtesy of T. A. Dorsett)

400 DOLLARS
REWARD.

ESCAPED on the morning of the 25th inst. from the Chambersburg Prison, the following persons, viz:

David Lewis,
The noted Counterfeiter and Robber!

Who is about 6 feet high, round shouldered, straight and well made, athletic and active; sandy hair and whiskers. He took with him a suit of blue cloth, considerably worn. A reward of *Three hundred dollars*, will be given for delivering him to the Keeper of the Chambersburg Prison.

Felix M'Guire,

An Irishman, about 5 feet 5 inches high, dark hair and pale in the face—He took with him a crossbarred check shirt, a Sailor's blue jacket, brown Holland pantaloons, an old hat and shoes. —A reward of 25 *Dollars* will be given for delivering him at the above mentioned place.

John Myers,

About 5 feet 6 inches high, stout built, about 25 years old.—He took with him a roundabout and pantaloons of bed-ticking, and an old hat.—A reward of 25 *Dollars* will be given for delivering him at the above mentioned place.

Caesar Rodney,

A Mulatto man about 5 feet 10 inches high, middle aged.—He took with him a pair of brown Holland pantaloons, check shirt, a pair of shoes and hat.—A reward of 25 *Dollars* will be given for delivering him at the above mentioned place.

Peter Pendleton,

A Negro, middle aged, 5 feet 6 or 7 inches high; slim made; lately lived with John Kynor of Green township.—He took with him a check shirt, blue roundabout and an old wool hat. —A reward of 25 *Dollars* will be given for delivering him at the above mentioned place.

Jeremiah Snider, *Sheriff*.

Chambersburg, May 29, 1820.

Detail *(right) of main door of Old Jail, Chambersburg, showing ancient lock and key.*

The Franklin County Jail (above) *was less than two years old when Cumberland county officials deemed it a stronger keep in which to lodge the notorious bandit David Lewis in* 1820 *But the newest, strongest prison in Pennsylvania could not contain the Commonwealth's Robin Hood. He and four fellow prisoners escaped from the jail on May* 25, 1820.

(AHA Photos by Sid Miller)

Only seven men have been hanged in Franklin county, Pa. The Franklin county gallows (above), once loaned to Washington county, Md., has been erected in the yard of the Old Jail, Chambersburg.

William F. Reed (right), of Mont Alto and Waynesboro, was the gallows' last victim, being hanged in 1912 for the murder of Sadie Hurley Mathna. He lies buried in Rose Hill Cemetery, Mont Alto.

(AHA Photo by Sid Miller)

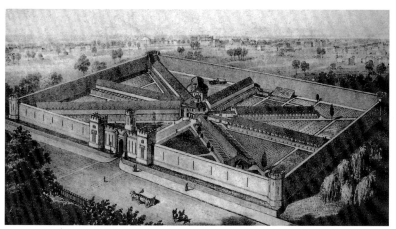

The world's first "penitentiary" was built at Philadelphia in 1829. *Eastern Penitentiary* (above) *was designed to advance the "Pennsylvania system" of incarceration, which stressed solitary confinement as a catalyst for spiritual rehabilitation, or penitence. This approach to imprisonment challenged the Auburn, or "New York," system, which embraced such methods as forced group labour in silence and physical punishment. While most of the United States favoured the Auburn system, Eastern became a model for hundreds of prisons around the world.*

Eastern housed such famous men as Al Capone and Willie Sutton; but it also sheltered some PSI topics of study: Henry Heist, Jacob Shockey, Samuel Shockey, John D. Lesher, and John H. Monn all spent time there.

When Eastern Penitentiary was built, Pennsylvania law required its warden to visit every prisoner on a daily basis, and guards needed to interact with each inmate three times every day. The prison's hub-and-spoke floor plan (right, as it appeared in 1836) *was intended to facilitate this regimen.*

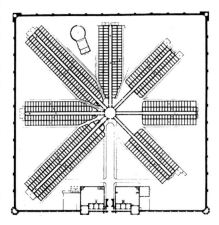

The Commonwealth abandoned Eastern in 1971, and it is now a museum.

ABOVE: *Brothers Jacob Emile Shockey (left;* 1895–1924*) and Samuel Thomas Shockey (*1899–1928*) both met their fates by gunshot wounds, but who was responsible for either of their deaths remains a bone of contention.* (Courtesy of Mr. Perry Price)

OPPOSITE PAGE: *Miss Iva Wills* alias *Iva Leggee* alias *Iva Shockey* alias *Iva Thoman (*1903–1980*), the flame-haired* femme fatale *who changed the Shockey boys' lives in the Spring of* 1924. (From *The Evening News*, Harrisburg, Pa., March 27, 1924)

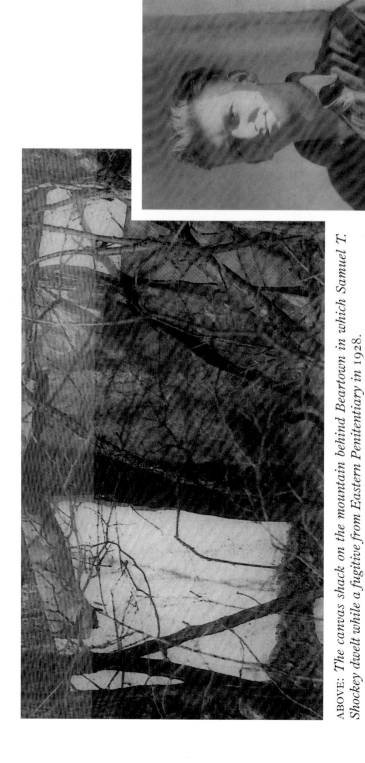

ABOVE: *The canvas shack on the mountain behind Beartown in which Samuel T. Shockey dwelt while a fugitive from Eastern Penitentiary in* 1928.

RIGHT: *"Sam" Shockey himself.* (Both courtesy of PSI Franklin J. Shockey)

OPPOSITE: *Corpse of "Sam" Shockey at Deer Lick Rock, near Beartown on February* 11, 1928. *Note absence of snow on trousers, supposedly pulled up and refastened by his brother Christian, who discovered the body. His murder remains officially unsolved.*

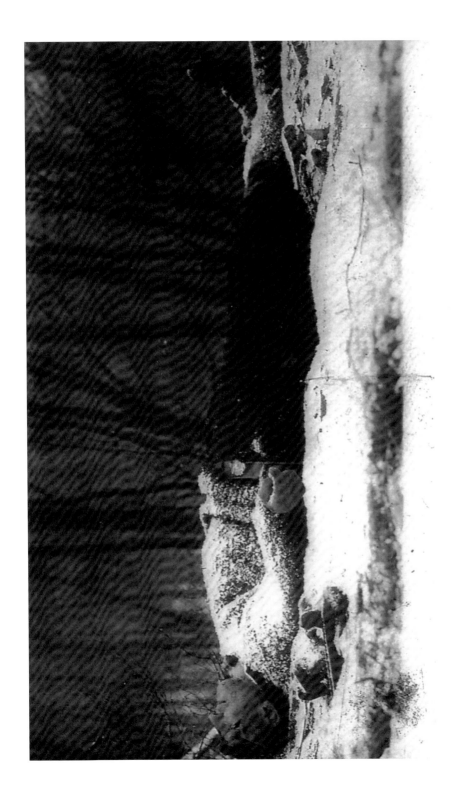

Gerard Rushton Peabody forsook a life of privilege to embark on a long, ironic career of criminal conduct. ABOVE: *Mrs. C. E. Peabody with her eight sons in a portrait by Curtis, Seattle, ca. 1915. "Jerry" is denoted by the arrow.*

Gerard R. Peabody (right) *in a passport photograph while residing in Australia, 1920.*

OPPOSITE PAGE: *Gerard "Uncle Jerry" Peabody* (left) *as he appeared when he sojourned in the Antietam country, robbing banks.*

The second Mrs. Gerard Peabody (upper right), nee *Ruth Hall, testified in Jerry's behalf at his Baltimore trial.*

Peabody built a one-room combination residence and shop (bottom right) *on the south side of Miltary road (Maryland Route 550) between Highfield and Sabillasville. It served as headquarters for his bank robbery ring.*

THE RECORD HERALD

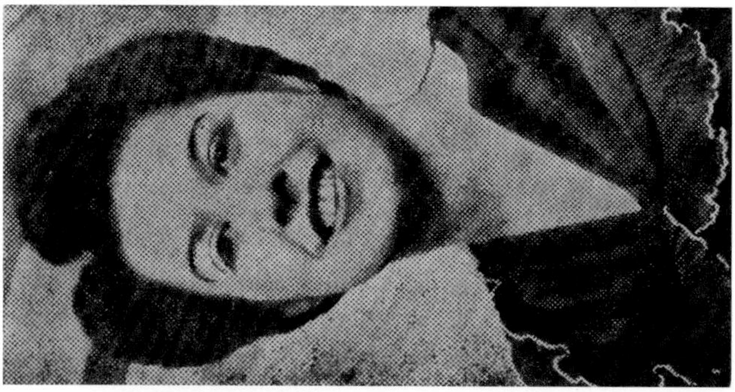

COURTESY OF FRANK BOCK

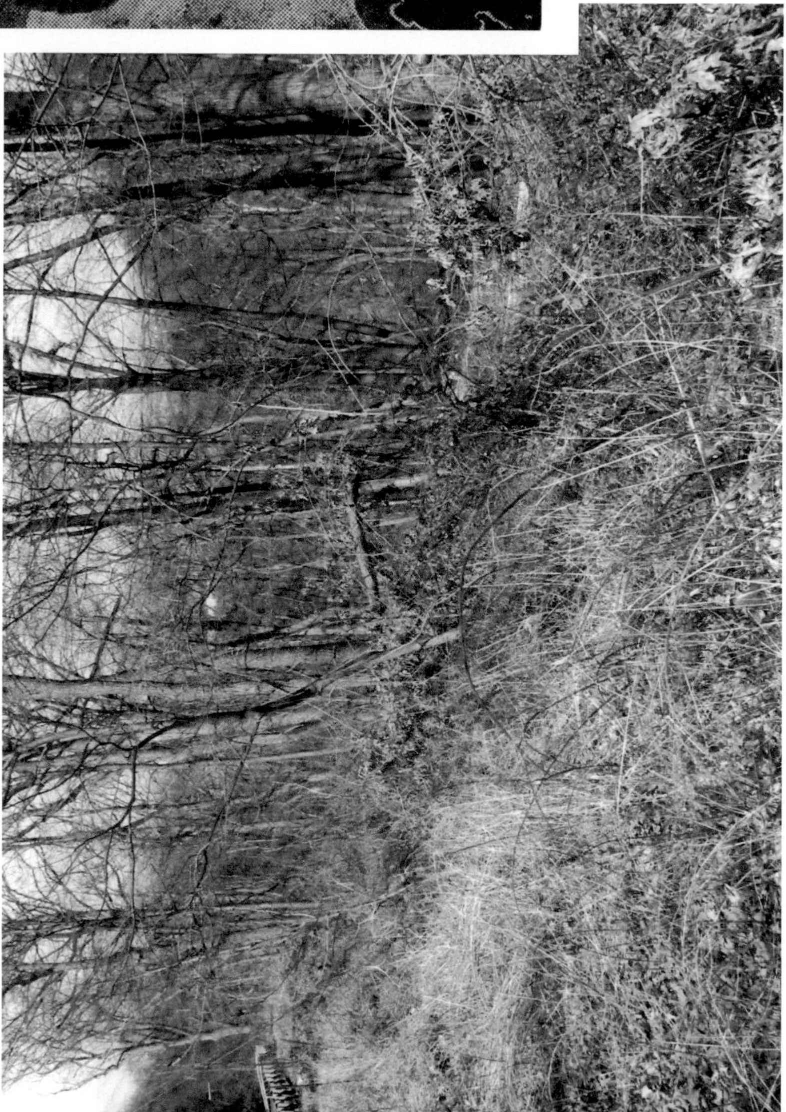

ABOVE: *The nearly nude body of Miss Betty Jane Kennedy (above right), of Hagerstown, Md., was found at this secluded spot on South Mountain near Rouzerville, Pa., on April 4, 1946. She had been garrotted and otherwise injured. Despite (or perhaps because of) the efforts of numerous law enforcement agencies, her murder remains one of the great American mysteries.* THE POTOMAC STREET IRREGULARS *intend to revisit the case annually in April.*

RIGHT: *Site near Buena Vista Springs, Pa., where a local resident, Mrs. Luther Mummert, found Miss Betty Jane Kennedy's pocketboot on the afternoon of April 4, 1946.*

119

THE POTOMAC STREET IRREGULARS.

Integral members of this Antietam Historical Association crime study group, the lead detectives who contributed to this volume are pictured at "History House," from left to right: PSIs Sue Lee, Todd Dorsett, Michael Logan, Frank Bock, Jim Shockey, and Tim Shockey.

(AHA Photo by Sid Miller)

VIII.
The Murder of Mrs. John Lesher.

FRANKLIN J. SHOCKEY.

August 13, 2013.

The eighth meeting of the Potomac Street Irregulars was held at the Parlor House. Thirty-one persons attended. PSI Franklin Shockey led the discussion about the first of two domestic shootings from downtown Waynesboro to be covered this year.

FANNIE Davis Lesher had a reputation as an unfaithful wife, and largely because of it her husband managed to kill her and escape a first-degree murder conviction. At the same time, the fact that John D. Lesher himself had a fairly good reputation as a responsible, even-tempered citizen did him no harm; and his case illustrates how juries will sometimes sympathize with a defendant when there are extenuating circumstances, regardless how intentional his wrongdoing.

On November 30, 1923, *The Record-Herald*'s top headline read,—

"JOHN D. LESHER SHOOTS AND KILLS WIFE."

The newspaper then recounted how, the previous afternoon, Thanksgiving Day, in downtown Waynesboro, Pennsylvania, John Lesher twice fired a 32-calibre Iver Johnson revolver at his estranged wife and killed her. Lesher readily confessed that he shot twice at his wife, but he had not been himself lately.

The incriminating facts of the Lesher murder case were straightforward and uncontested. Rather, the issue facing the jury concerned John Lesher's mental state at the time he shot his wife shortly after two o'clock in the afternoon, Thursday, November 29, 1923.

Fannie Lesher was born in Maryland on July 4, 1898. She was

a daughter of Thomas and Lillie (Hahn) Davis, who settled at Waynesboro when Fannie was young.[1] Her father was a long-time employee of Anson W. Good in his fuel business, and was also a janitor at the Citizens National Bank, Waynesboro.[2]

John D. Lesher was born in Quincy township, Franklin county, on July 17, 1887. He was a son of Jeremiah R. and Mary G. (Hovis) Lesher.[3] His father worked as a machinist in one of the factories at Waynesboro.

Fannie and John Lesher had been married around seven years when they signed articles of marital separation and parted. Not long before that, Fannie had gone to keep house for a widower, Elmer E. Potts, who had a teenage daughter, Pauline, at home. John Lesher had been boarding at his mother's residence on West North street, Waynesboro, since he and his wife separated.

Fannie had a total of four offspring, three of whom appear to have been the issue of John Lesher. Upon the Leshers' separation, the two sons, Carl Woodrow Schrader and Harry D. Lesher, remained with their grandparents Davis, who dwelt in Mulberry avenue, Waynesboro, at the rear of 34 South Church Street; daughter Geraldine M. Lesher went to live with her aunt Lottie Davis Schrader, near Philadelphia; and two-year-old May Lesher lived with her mother at Potts's.

John Lesher visited the Potts home that Thursday to talk to his wife. He followed Elmer Potts into the house, where the two men and Fannie treated briefly before Lesher began accusing Potts of causing the difficulty between his wife and him. Potts then withdrew to Center square, leaving the Leshers alone in the house. During the ensuing argument between Fannie and John, the latter fired two shots in the direction of his wife, probably as she attempted to exit the house by the back door. According to the coroner's investigation, one of the bullets from the revolver "had entered the body from the back, under the right shoulder blade, crossing diagonally and through the right ventricle of the heart. The bullet was found in the left breast."[4]

---

[1] Commonwealth of Pennsylvania Certificate of Death #117164.

[2] *The Record Herald* (Waynesboro, Pa.), July 30, 1946, p. 8, col. 3.

[3] Commonwealth of Pennsylvania Certificate of Death #95765.

[4] "John D. Lesher Shoots and Kills Wife," *The Record-Herald*, p. 1, col. 7; p. 2,

The Potts residence was a rented frame house located in the first block of East Gay street (commonly referred to as "Gas alley"). It stood at the end of the lot of Dr. Nevie C. Detrich (now occupied by Mr. John P. Leos and The Candy Kitchen). Mrs. Lesher's parents dwelt around the corner, in another alley dwelling. Fannie's son Carl,[5] aged about eight years, was walking along South Church street near the intersection with Gay street when he heard the report of two shots from the direction of the Potts house. He turned in his tracks and as he approached the Potts place, he met John Lesher, who told him not to go back to Potts's, for no one was there. Carl went to the Potts house anyway and found his mother lying in the yard near the back porch with her two-year-old daughter May at her feet. The boy began screaming. He ran towards his home and told the first person he saw on the street what had happened, and that he had met John Lesher walking away from the scene. His grandmother Davis accompanied him back to Potts's.

By this time, other residents who had heard the boy screaming had converged on Potts's. They included men who had been working on the F. E. Grove house two doors away at 27 South Church street, and auctioneer A. D. Adams and his son Herbert, who dwelt at 23 South Church Street, just across Gay street from the Potts residence. Mrs. Davis took care of little May Lesher, whom the men had found lying across her mother's feet. About ten minutes after Carl discovered his mother's body, the Waynesboro police arrived on the scene. The police attempted unsuccessfully to contact Franklin County Coroner J. H. Kinter, so after about an hour, the officers moved Mrs. Lesher's body to the nearby Grove funeral establishment because rain had begun to fall. The coroner later endorsed the officers' removal of the body.

Meanwhile, John Lesher had walked directly to his mother's

---

col. 3.

[5] Carl Woodrow Schrader (1915–1943) was the son of Fannie Davis and Carl Nelson Schrader. Fannie's sister Lottie was the first wife of Carl N. Schrader's brother Joseph M. Schrader. During service in the Second World War, the boy who found his mother lying shot was killed when the ship on which he served, the tanker *MS Atlantic Sun*, was torpedoed one hundred fifty miles off Cape Rice, Newfoundland.

house. There he told her and a neighbour, Walter Bryan, that he had shot Fannie. At that time, he placed his weapon on the kitchen table. Bryan advised Lesher to surrender to police, so Lesher started walking toward borough hall. Bryan caught up with him near the Leland hotel, and as the two embarked toward the police station, they met Chief of Police Byers and Patrolman W. Fred Gillan who had started for the Lesher home to arrest Lesher. He offered no resistance when arrested.

News of the tragedy spread quickly, and a large crowd of spectators assembled around the Potts house until they heard that Lesher was seen walking towards central Waynesboro; then the crowd hurried toward the Square to witness his arrest.

Thursday evening, at seven o'clock, Magistrate L. S. Kepner arraigned John D. Lesher on the charge of murder and committed him to jail. En route to Chambersburg, Lesher said little other than that the revolver used in the shooting came from a taxicab. When Chief Byers confiscated the weapon, two of its five chambers were empty.

The same evening, Dr. Kinter, assisted by Waynesboro physicians Drs. A. Barr Snively and D. M. Shoemaker, performed an autopsy on Mrs. Lesher's body. Their findings are set forth above.

The police investigation immediately disclosed that Lesher had visited the Potts's around seven o'clock in the morning on Thanksgiving Day; that both he and Fannie had been at her parents' in the morning, quarreling, and that Lesher had been drinking and had whiskey in his possession at the Davis place. The police noted that there was evidence that Lesher had been drinking when they arrested him, but that he was not intoxicated.

At eleven o'clock Friday morning, the coroner held his inquest at the Grove Funeral Home. The jurors empanelled were Smith W. Cunningham, W. H. Morrison, J. A. Knupp, Walter E. K. Miller, Wilbur Kauffman, and E. E. Conrad. Franklin County District Attorney Clippinger cross-examined the witnesses.

At the inquest, Motter Thompson testified that Carl Schrader's screams had drawn him to the Potts place, where he found Mrs. Lesher lying on the walk at the rear of the house. He called Dr. D. M. Shoemaker and the police.

Walter Bryan, who resided in the other side of the duplex in which Lesher and his mother dwelt, testified that he, his wife, and their daughter, Ethel, were drawn next door by the elder Mrs. Lesher's screams and those of her granddaughter Mary Hess. Mrs. Lesher related to Bryan how her son had told her he shot his wife. Lesher himself told Bryan that he had shot twice at Fannie, but he was not sure whether both bullets struck her. Bryan then took the revolver from the kitchen table, advised Lesher to surrender to authorities, and followed the beleaguered man in the direction of police headquarters. Bryan was with Lesher when police arrested him.

Dr. Shoemaker testified that, except for the effects of the bullet, Mrs. Fannie Lesher's physical condition was perfect. He also noted that there were no signs of a struggle.

Elmer Potts testified that Mrs. Lesher had been keeping his house for two months, and retold the facts of his encounter with Lesher immediately prior to the shooting.

Mrs. Fannie Lesher's elder son, Carl W. Schrader, testified that he heard two shots while passing in front of the Stickell residence.[6] He noted that the sounds seemed to come from the Potts place. As he continued towards the Potts house, about halfway between Church street and the house, he met John Lesher, who had exited the Potts yard by a gate. Carl then ran around to the rear of the house and found his mother as aforesaid.

Chief Byers testified about hearing of the shooting while he and Patrolman Gillan were in northern Waynesboro, about going to the scene, and about arresting Lesher.

The coroner's jury then rendered this verdict:

"We the undersigned jurors in the case of Mrs. Fannie M. Lesher, find that the said Fannie M. Lesher came to her death on November 29 at Waynesboro from a bullet wound inflicted by John Lesher by means of a revolver."[7]

Fannie Davis Lesher's remains were buried in Green Hill Cemetery, Waynesboro.[8]

---

[6] 19 South Church Street, located on the northeast corner of Church and Gay streets.

[7] "John D. Lesher Shoots and Kills Wife," p. 2, cols. 3–4.

[8] Commonwealth of Pennsylvania Certificate of Death #117164.

Spectators jammed the courtroom on February 6, 1924, for the opening of John D. Lesher's murder trial. They strained to see the defendant, while newspapermen noted his "shifting gaze" as he sat beside his counsel. Otherwise, his face showed no emotion except when the district attorney announced that he intended to prove that Lesher had acted "willfully, deliberately, premeditatedly and with malice aforethought." At those words, Lesher showed signs of mental stress as his forehead glistened with sweat.

At trial, the first prosecution witness was Dr. Shoemaker. He testified that, having been called to the Potts home, he found Mrs. Lesher dead, lying on her left side on the ground. There were blood clots on her face and hands. A powder burn showed on the back of her blue-and-white dotted dress, through which a hole had been pierced to a corresponding hole in her body below the right shoulder blade. The body exhibited no other wounds, and the only blood visible had come from her nose and mouth. The doctor could not identify the bullet shown him at trial as the one he had removed from the body, although he said the two were similar.[9]

Elmer E. Potts essentially recounted the facts he had provided the police and the coroner's jury. He noted that he had known Lesher many years, and had known Fannie since she was a child. He testified that, when Lesher followed him into the house on Thanksgiving afternoon, he sat down and, after making accusations to Potts, asked his wife, "Fanny, are you going to live with me?" Potts quoted Fannie as replying, "I can't talk to you now, you've been drinking!" She encouraged Potts to leave because she anticipated a quarrel with Lesher. Potts admitted that he never heard Lesher threaten Fannie.

Fannie's son Carl, described as a "10-year-old towheaded lad," noted, in addition to what he had declared at earlier proceedings, that his mother was not dead when he arrived at Potts's, but that she breathed her last shortly after he arrived.

Motter Thompson testified that he heard Carl's screams and

---

[9] "Lesher Bares Home Troubles, Accuses Wife," *The Record-Herald*, February 7, 1924, p. 1, col. 7.

went toward the alley. Herbert Adams was at the gate to the Potts yard, and called to him, "Come here quick." Thompson testified that when he arrived in the yard, the child May was walking around, while her mother's corpse lay across the brick path. He placed May on the porch, and an "old lady" emerged from the house and took charge of her. Thompson then called Dr. Shoemaker.

Walter Bryan testified that he was the elder Mrs. Lesher's next-door neighbour; that he heard a woman scream, then moan, and then call, "Mr. Bryan come over." He jumped over the back fence, and his daughter followed him. Inside Mrs. Lesher's they found John Lesher, his mother, and his niece Mary Hess. Lesher stated, "I've shot Fan and killed her. I don't know whether the second shot took effect or not."

Bryan further testified that his daughter asked Lesher, "Why did you do it?" Lesher replied simply, "My troubles were too great."

Bryan then seized the revolver from the kitchen table, and later gave it to Lesher's brother Harry. He advised Lesher to quiet himself and stop upsetting his mother. Lesher then left to surrender to authorities. Bryan met him at the Leland hotel and offered to accompany him to the police station. En route they met Chief Byers, who arrested Lesher and removed a homemade blackjack from his right-hand overcoat pocket. Bryan also stated that Lesher declared that Elmer Potts was to blame for his marital trouble.

Ethel Bryan corroborated her father's testimony. She stated that when she entered the Lesher residence, Mrs. Lesher said, "John shot Fan."

Police traced the revolver used in the shooting to a Wishard taxicab which Lesher had engaged on Thanksgiving Day. Cab driver John Kauffman first took Lesher to his brother's house in Lincoln avenue, thence to his mother's, and finally to the vicinity of the Potts residence. Before exiting the taxi, Lesher asked Kauffman how much he would charge to take Lesher and Fannie to Philadelphia. Kauffman quoted a fare of fifty dollars, and Lesher responded that he would talk to his wife about it.

Kauffman had placed the revolver in the right-hand pocket of the taxicab after Robert Wishard, son of owner Roy Wishard, had given it to him to take to the Wishard home whenever he was in its vicinity. Later on Thanksgiving Day, they found the gun missing from the taxicab.[10]

On February 7, John D. Lesher took the witness stand in his own defense. He testified that marital troubles had haunted him since early in 1922 but vanished suddenly when he fired a bullet into his wife at Potts's house. The Waynesboro newspaper summarized his lament:

"Deception, infidelity and immorality all played leading roles in Lesher's domestic tragedy. He said his wife went out on an automobile party with two men and another girl; at another time she arrived home at 1 o'clock in the morning and crawled through a rear window. Her breath smelled of liquor, Lesher said. Lesher stated neighbors reported that men visited his home in his absence, and at one time he 'caught' a man coming from his home. At another time, he said, his wife became ill. Physicians said she had a 'disease,' Lesher said. After she recovered from the trouble which confined her to her home she returned and later 'got the same thing again.'"[11]

Taking the stand confidently, John Lesher related that he was born at Quincy, a son of Jere and Mary Lesher. At the age of twelve years he left home to live with his aunt on a farm one mile from Mont Alto on the road leading to Altenwald. While there, he attended Webster school. At the age of fourteen, he went to live with his uncle Michael Helman for two seasons. Then, when seventeen years old, he came to Waynesboro and secured employment with the Emmert Manufacturing Company. Later he moved to the farm of his uncle Crawford Helman, Altenwald, staying there one summer and one winter. Returning to Waynesboro, he went to work at the Geiser plant.

John Lesher was married twice, being divorced from his first wife. After marrying Fannie Davis, they dwelt on the Hess farm for a few months, then boarded with her parents for a year before

---

[10] *Ibid.* at p. 8, col. 3.
[11] *Ibid.*

going to housekeeping on their own account at Waynesboro.[12]

The defense was attempting to show that accounts of Fannie's unfaithfulness and neglect of his children had caused Lesher to become despondent and mentally unstable by the time he confronted his wife at Potts's on Thanksgiving Day. The district attorney objected to this line of questioning; however, Judge Gillan ruled that, because a life might be at stake, he would permit the defense to continue, provided they first proved Lesher's state of mind at the time of the shooting. Then, he ruled, the defense could offer evidence of what caused that state of mind.[13]

Miss Pauline Potts testified that she was present at Davis's the night before Thanksgiving Day and heard Lesher exclaim, "Fanny will not be at 'Dude' Potts' house next week this time." Mrs. Davis and Fannie were also present when he made that statement.

Fannie's mother, "an elderly, careworn, somberly-dressed woman," corroborated the Potts girl's testimony. Her lips trembled and she shielded her eyes with her hands as she sobbed audibly when shown part of the dress Fannie had been wearing when she was shot. She identified it as Fannie's.

Fannie's sister Miss Catherine Davis testified that on the Monday before Thanksgiving Day, she had heard Lesher state that he would have "Fanny away from Potts before the week was over."

Harry Lesher testified that Walter Bryan had given him the revolver and cartridges, and that he later surrendered them to the Waynesboro police.

Patrolman Gillan attested to Bryan's delivery of the empty revolver shells, and to the surrender of the weapon, which he identified in court. Chief Byers testified about the details of Lesher's arrest, including finding the homemade blackjack in his overcoat pocket. Byers said he asked Lesher why he had committed the act, and that his prisoner replied, "My troubles were too great."[14]

One important circumstance disclosed during Chief Byers's testimony was that Lesher told him that John Kauffman had

---

[12] The 1920 Federal Decennial Census lists the Leshers as residing at 110 Middle Street, Waynesboro.

[13] *Ibid.*

[14] *Ibid.*

driven him to John Sharer's place at Roadside to obtain a quart of whiskey. Sharer was not at home, so Lesher looked through the taxicab for something to read while waiting, and found the revolver. On his way to the county jail, Lesher asked Byers whether Fannie was dead. But he neither admitted nor denied shooting her. The chief added that, on Thanksgiving Day, Lesher "looked like the morning after the night before."[15]

Cab driver Nevin Thompson testified that he received a call to pick up a fare at the Leland hotel. Upon his arrival there, Lesher emerged from the lobby and, assuming that Thompson had heard what he had done, asked whether Fannie was dead. After Thompson replied that that was the general belief, Lesher dismissed him, saying that he would walk to the police station.

Former coroner Dr. J. H. Kinter identified the bullet removed from Fannie Lesher's body during the autopsy. Then the prosecution rested its case.

So great was the interest in the Lesher trial that many of the spectators did not leave the courtroom to eat lunch. John Lesher resumed his testimony at 2:15 P.M. He noted that he had consulted Judge Gillan some time before the shooting regarding Fannie's conduct. The judge referred him to the district attorney.[16]

The basis of Lesher's defense was that he was in a "dazed mental condition" when his wife was shot. He claimed that the daze seized him while he sat in the front room of the Potts house. Something scraped his knuckles, then something struck him in the head, and the next thing he knew he was retrieving his revolver and cap from the floor. He asserted that he then left the house. He did not see or think of his wife, nor did he remember seeing his stepson Carl in the alley. He went to the rear of the Benedict building[17] and became quite sick. He claimed he was not normal mentally for two weeks thereafter.

Lesher further asserted that on Thanksgiving Day, John Kauffman had driven him to Sharer's at Roadside, where he purchased a quart of whiskey for eight dollars, of which Kauffman contrib-

---

[15] *Ibid.*
[16] *Ibid.*
[17] 18 West Main Street, since demolished.

uted fifty cents. Then Kauffman took one drink, and Lesher took several. Then he shared his whiskey with some friends, and took several more drinks himself. This left him with about a pint of whiskey. Then he met with John Flautt and walked with him a short distance before going to Wishard's poolroom, where he again met Kauffman. He then engaged Kauffman's cab for a ride around town, ending near the Potts residence, where the negotiations about a trip to Philadelphia occurred. At Potts's, Lesher alleged, he wanted to talk to his wife about their son, who was suffering from diphtheria.[18]

Lesher attempted to refute the testimony of Pauline Potts and his sister-in-law by claiming that the statements he had made about Fannie's not being with Potts a week hence referred to the intended trip to Philadelphia.

Lesher explained that the blackjack taken from his pocket when he was arrested was protection against a "gang" from Greencastle who had threatened him. He likewise claimed that he had taken the revolver for the purpose of protecting himself from the same Greencastle gang.

The defendant testified that, on one occasion after he and his wife had signed articles of separation, Fannie had shown him a handful of money she said she had made by "misconduct." His testimony ended at half past three o'clock in the afternoon of February 7.

Other witnesses testified about Fannie Lesher's reputation and relationships with other men. Among those testifying were Mrs. Percy Robinson, Walter Ambrose, Stuart Foster, Robert McCleaf, Frank Foster, Lester Clopper, and Gail Noll.

Harry Watson testified that he was one of the friends who drank with Lesher on Thanksgiving Day, and John Flautt stated that Lesher was intoxicated when he walked with him that afternoon.

Numerous other witnesses testified regarding John Lesher's mental state immediately prior to Fannie's shooting, and to John's reputation as a peaceful and quiet resident of Waynes-

---

[18] "Dazed Mental Condition is Lesher's Plea" *The Record-Herald*, February 8, 1924, p. 1, col. 7.

boro. Auctioneer A. D. Adams stated that Lesher's reputation was good, although he had heard of Lesher's striking Fannie. D. C. Bonebrake, William Middour, Thomas Cook, "Squire" Culler, and Anson W. Good (Lesher's employer) all testified as to Lesher's good reputation.

Dr. Robert B. Brown testified that he had attended Fannie Lesher when her child was born in July 1921, and that he had treated her for a communicable disease in August 1922.

Stuart Foster recalled that John Lesher had refused a cash settlement from a man who allegedly had paid attention to Fanny the summer before her death.[19]

As for Lesher's state of mind on Thanksgiving Day: C. M. Barr saw Lesher at the Leland hotel and followed him down the opposite side of the street as he walked toward borough hall. The witness noted that Lesher "looked like a child being led" and "like a man in a dream."

The former magistrate who had arraigned Lesher on the murder charge, L. S. Kepner, said that when he asked Lesher whether he was guilty, the defendant said he "hardly knew what had happened." Sometime later, Lesher asked, "Did this happen in the day time or at night?"

Patrolman Gillan testified that Lesher showed signs of having been drinking on the day of the shooting.

Mrs. Harry Lesher confirmed that John Lesher had been acting peculiar prior to Fannie's death. She testified that Lesher had wanted her to visit his wife, but she resisted. When she finally relented, Lesher said to her, "Now, talk nice to her, don't be ugly." The witness said she considered that "soft" talk for a man. She also recounted how he would nurse his son to sleep and gaze intensely into the child's eyes for lengthy periods.

The defendant's brother Daniel Lesher also testified to John's peculiar behaviour, noting that the prisoner would "talk at length on subjects with which Daniel said he knew John was not familiar. At times he would sit with his head in cupped hands like a man greatly worried."

---

[19] "Dazed Mental Condition is Lesher's Plea," *The Record-Herald*, February 8, 1924, p. 4, col. 4.

"Squire" Culler, a magistrate, testified that Lesher had called at his office and said, "I don't know what in the name of God to do. I found my children in a dark street. . . . I found Fanny where the children said. With another man. I want you to write a notice to both of them." When Lesher apprised Culler that the two had received their notices, he paid the costs and asked the magistrate not to say who had requested the notices.

Dr. Samuel B. Thomas had observed that, for a month or more prior to Thanksgiving Day, John Lesher had not been mentally sound. Lesher often had hallucinations which sometimes amounted to a sort of mania.[20]

Dr. Kinter was recalled to rebut Dr. Brown's testimony. He stated that the disease for which Dr. Brown alleged he treated Fannie Lesher would have left traces in her body, but that during the autopsy he found no evidence that she had had such an illness.

Dr. Brown was recalled to defend his position. He testified that the disease in question does not necessarily leave traces in one's body after treatment. And, indeed, Dr. Kinter had to concede that he had not examined Fannie Lesher's brain during the autopsy.

The Commonwealth called a number of witnesses to testify that Lesher was sane on Thanksgiving Day. They included Elmer Potts, John H. Kauffman, Pauline Potts, policeman Stephen W. Staley, Nevin Thompson, Frank Mace, Jacob A. Cline, John D. Sanders, Adam Kauffman, and Chief Byers.

Of course, none of these witnesses was an expert. During cross-examination, defense attorney Edmund C. Wingerd asked Cline what an "insane man" was. The witness responded that he had seen such persons in an insane asylum. In this answer, defense counsel obtained precisely what he sought.[21] No further examination was necessary.

The Commonwealth summoned Dr. J. C. Greenawalt as an expert on insanity. He refuted Dr. Thomas's assertion that John

---

[20] *Ibid.*, col. 5.
[21] "Lesher's Fate Soon will be in Hands of Jury," *The Record-Herald*, February 9, 1924, p. 1, col. 7; p. 6, col. 4.

Lesher was not wholly sane. Dr. Greenawalt stated that the evidence produced at trial as well as Lesher's family history and personality traits disclosed nothing suggesting insanity.

On the issue of intoxication, Dr. Greenawalt noted that the evidence showed that Lesher had consumed only a small portion of a quart of whiskey. Consuming that amount of alcohol, he opined, would not result in "aggravated intoxication."[22]

Upon close of the evidence and arguments, the court briefly instructed the jury. Judge Gillan told the jurors that they had four verdicts from which to choose: guilty of first-degree murder, guilty of second-degree murder, guilty of manslaughter, or not guilty.

In the evening on February 9, after slightly less than four hours' deliberation, the jury returned a verdict: John D. Lesher WAS GUILTY OF MURDER IN THE SECOND DEGREE. The prisoner sat calmly as he heard the words saving him from the death penalty. "There was not the flicker of an eye-lid or the twitching of a muscle to betray any emotion he may have felt. Neatly dressed, clean shaven and with lips pursed closely together he sat with eyes fixed on the clerk until the reading of the verdict was finished. He then held a brief whispered consultation with John W. Hoke, who with Edmund C. Wingerd, ably defended him at the trial."[23]

Defense counsel made no motion for a new trial. Accordingly, the district attorney moved for sentencing. Judge Gillan imposed the maximum possible penalty for murder in the second degree. He sentenced John D. Lesher to serve no less than ten years, nor more than twenty years, in Eastern Penitentiary, Philadelphia, to commence immediately. Newspaper accounts noted that Lesher remained calm throughout the proceedings, and reported that he was contented with his sentence.[24]

The murder of Fannie Davis Lesher occurred during Prohibi-

---

[22] *Ibid.*

[23] "Remains Calm as Jury Gives Guilty Verdict," *The Record-Herald*, February 11, 1924, p. 1, col. 7.

[24] "Lesher Given 10 to 20 Years," *The Record-Herald*, February 13, 1924, p. 1, col. 6.

tion. The Volstead act of 1919, which prohibited the manufacture and sale of alcoholic beverages beginning in January 1920, created a proliferation of criminal and dangerous activity. The surreptitious distillation of "moonshine" or "bootleg whiskey" often created a lethal product; sometimes it was merely harmful. Despite the jury's belief that John Lesher was of sound mind on Thanksgiving Day 1923, there is the possibility that he had been consuming illegal whiskey for some time, and that it had impaired his mental faculties.

Obviously something caused the jury to avoid a verdict of murder in the first degree. Even today questions linger in the minds of students of this case. Had Fannie been unfaithful? Had John abused her? Had Dr. Brown in fact treated Fannie for a sexually-transmitted disease? If so, would it necessarily have left traces in her body? Why had Dr. Kinter not examined Fannie's brain during the autopsy? Did someone indeed strike John Lesher on the head at Potts's that fateful day? And just how much illegal whiskey had John consumed before his final visit with Fannie? Or had John Lesher concocted his story to save himself from the electric chair?

These questions likely will never be answered. At all events, a woman lost her life, a man lost his liberty for at least ten years, and four small children were left without parental guidance.

Languishing in the bowels of Eastern Penitentiary, John D. Lesher submitted an application for a pardon, to be considered at the sitting of the Board of Pardons on April 22, 1930.[25] It appears the application was denied, for he is among the prisoners enumerated in the Philadelphia stronghold in the 1930 Federal Decennial Census.

Eventually John Lesher did gain release from prison. He returned to Waynesboro, where he worked as a restaurant cook. He died November 3, 1946, at the home of his brother Daniel, and lies buried in the Antietam Cemetery (Price's Church grave-

---

[25] "Local Man One of Eight Seeking Pardon This Week," *The Record-Herald*, April 21, 1930, p. 8, col. 2.

yard).[26] Fannie's nephew Monroe Davis acted as one of John's pallbearers.[27]

---

[26] Commonwealth of Pennsylvania Certificate of Death #95765.
[27] *The Record Herald*, November 7, 1946, p. 12, col. 3.

IX.
The Shooting of Mrs. John Monn.

FRANK BOCK.

September 10, 2013.

The ninth meeting of the Potomac Street Irregulars was held at the Parlor House. Twenty-five persons attended. With wry wit, PSI Frank Bock introduced the use of "props" for greater illumination of the topic during PSI lectures. For his information about the case, he relied on newspaper accounts and a monograph prepared by the late Orville Monn.

HE tragedy climaxing in the death of Mrs. John H. Monn included quite a cast of characters. There was the drunken husband, the cheating wife, an array of male boarders with varying degrees of intimacy with the cheating wife, the meddling friends, the enabling mother, the onlookers who preferred not to get involved, doctors, lawyers, and an orphaned son.

The situation comprised fighting, cheating, drinking, attempted suicide, and murder. It involved guns, knives, razors,—and blood, lots of blood. And the conflicting stories about the affair were many, with witnesses sometimes contradicting themselves.

John Harry Monn was a self-described "common laborer" born January 18, 1879, in Quincy township, a son of Jacob and Alice (Creager) Monn. Molly V. (Kinley) Monn was born July 16, 1884, likewise in Quincy township, a daughter of Thomas J. and Lida A. (Welsh) Kinley. Both mothers were still living at the time of the murder.

To understand fully the importance of this case, one must first know what occurred in North Franklin street, Waynesboro, in the wee hours of October 5, 1913. The *Waynesboro Record* gave its customary treatment:

"John Monn, North Franklin street, made a brutal attack on his wife at his home and afterwards on the street, early Sunday morning, and severely injured her, cutting a deep gash in her arm with his knife, choking her and tearing her clothing.

"Other weapons that he tried to use on her were an ax and a razor. Miss Stouffer, who was with her in her room, got the ax from the infuriated man's hands and Mrs. Monn herself tore the razor from his fingers and tossed it into the street, where it was later found by Patrolman Harris.

"Monn, who is a tall and strong man, was maddened with jealousy and drink, it is said, and declared his intention of killing not only his wife but the three children in the house and several other occupants.

"He returned home after midnight. His wife was in a room with Miss Stouffer. The door was locked and, when Monn could not gain admission, he called first to his wife and then to Miss Stouffer to open the door.

"They refused and he battered in the door with an ax which he had carried to the second story.

"Brandishing the ax he advanced upon his wife, threatening to kill her, Mrs. Monn says. She caught hold of the ax and struggled with him to prevent his using it. Miss Stouffer came to her rescue and pulled the ax out of his hand.

"Monn was apparently well provided with weapons, for, when he lost the ax, he drew a razor. With that in his left hand, he rushed at his wife, caught her about the neck with his right hand, and slashed at her with the razor. She managed to avoid being cut and then got the razor out of his hand and threw it out the window.

"Angered now more than ever, Monn dragged his wife from the room and part of the way down the stairs. She caught hold of the balustrade and not only checked him but pulled him back into the room and to the foot of the bed.

"Here he drew his knife and cut his wife in the left arm, with his knife.

"'I'll cut your throat or your heart out!' he shouted, Mrs. Monn says.

"As he struck at her chest with the knife, she threw up her left arm and the knife blade sank into it.

"Her brother, Horace Kenley,[1] appeared at this time and knocked him down with a chair.

"Mrs. Monn escaped from the house and started to run up Franklin street toward North. Her husband pursued and caught her and although she, on her knees, begged him not to continue to harm her, he threw her to the ground, and was beating her when a neighbor, attracted by the noise, discharged his revolver into the air and

---

[1] Harris W. Kinley.

declared he'd shoot Monn, if he didn't desist from his attack on his wife.

"Monn looked up at this and his wife managed to escape from him and find a refuge in a nearby house. All this occurred between 3 and 4 o'clock."[2]

John Monn escaped into the night but was later arrested at his mother's residence at Tomstown. The grand jury found a true bill against him for aggravated assault and battery;[3] but at trial the jury had no choice but to acquit him because Mrs. Monn had disappeared from Waynesboro and could not be found, and without her testimony, the Commonwealth could not make a case against Monn.[4]

Three years later, "John Monn and family" were moving from Bonneauville, Adams county, Pennsylvania, to Waynesboro, "where they intend to make their future home."[5]

No one said it would be a happy home. After returning to Waynesboro, Molly and John Monn conducted boarding houses. The first of these was on East Main street near Hollinger avenue. Thence they moved to 17 East Main Street, where their ultimate struggle would occur. These are the essential facts of the murder:

"A double tragedy occurred Saturday morning at 5:30 o'clock at 17 East Main street when John Monn shot his wife, Molly (Kinnely) Monn, in the stomach with one shell from a 12-guage double barreled shot gun, and then turned the gun on himself, the shot penetrating the left side of his abdomen. He then, in order to insure the ending of his life, drew a pen knife from his pocket and thrust it deep in his throat, severing a vein which bled profusely.

"Mrs. Monn died about five minutes after he had shot her while he remained conscious and held up wonderfully after inflicting the terrible wounds to himself."[6]

---

[2] "John Monn Stabs Wife with Knife," *Waynesboro Record* (Waynesboro, Pa.), October 8, 1916, p. 8, col. 3. *See also* "Shoots Wife, Then Tries to Kill Himself," *The Evening News* (Harrisburg, Pa.), March 2, 1918, p. 1.

[3] *Waynesboro Record*, December 3, 1913, p. 5, col. 4.

[4] *Ibid.*, December 10, 1913, p. 7, col. 4.

[5] *Adams County News*, March 25, 1916, p. 4, col. 4.

[6] "Kills His Wife with Shot Gun, Shoots Self and Cuts Throat," *Waynesboro Record*, March 6, 1918, p. 1, col. 6. Some newspaper items give the address of the

At the time of the shooting, the Monn household consisted of Molly, John, and their ten-year-old adopted son, Cletus Monn; Molly's mother, Mrs. Thomas J. Kinley; Clyde Weyant, an employee of the CG&W Street Railway Company; J. Rush Johns, a Waynesboro policeman; Henry Kniss, Carl Steckman, Marvin Manningham, Charles Shaffer, and Samuel Shindle and his wife, Alice.

The shotgun blasts roused the boarders in the house, and several of them went downstairs to investigate. Johns and Weyant found John Monn lying on the dining room floor, shot and bleeding, and Molly on the kitchen floor, shot and dying, with the shotgun near her feet. She said, "Mr. Johns, I'm dying."

Johns and Weyant ignored John Monn, and carried Molly to a sofa in a dining room, where she died shortly thereafter. After going downstairs and seeing Johns and Weyant standing beside Molly's body on the sofa, Steckman went for a doctor, but could find none at home; so he sent his friend Kniss, whom he met on the street, to call Dr. J. W. Croft, who arrived shortly after Mrs. Monn died. Acting as a representative for Franklin County Coroner J. H. Kinter, Croft determined that Molly died as the result of "Hemorrhage from gunshot wound. Shot by her husband in groin, died before I arrived." He estimated that she had died five minutes after being shot.[7]

Dr. Croft rendered John Monn what surgical aid he could to arrest the weakened man's bleeding, and then Steckman accompanied Monn to the Chambersburg Hospital on the seven o'clock trolley. Upon Monn's arrival at the hospital, at half past eight, Coroner Kinter and Justice of the Peace Van T. Haulman took his statement. Monn acknowledged shooting his wife and himself, but he denied cutting his own throat and placing a razor in his pocket. The razor, he said, was not his. Instead, he accused Weyant of inflicting the wounds to his throat while he lay on the dining room floor.

Monn also accused Weyant of being the chief cause of the trouble between Molly and him. He claimed that, after the shooting,

---

Monn boarding house as 72 East Main Street.
[7] Commonwealth of Pennsylvania Death Certificate #32734.

"tramped out" Monn's brains.

Monn also later accused Shaffer of being intimate with Molly six to eight months beforehand. He had found a letter from Molly to Shaffer, which aroused his jealousy. As had happened five years previously, Monn began drinking heavily, which aggravated his rage.

Coroner Kinter empanelled a jury consisting of David Kauffman, Walter E. K. Miller, G. Ed. Crall, F. W. Benedict, W. H. Morrison, and John A. Potter, and held an inquest at borough hall, across the street from the scene of the murder. Their verdict: "That Mrs. Mollie Monn came to her death on the second day of March by reason of gunshot wounds at the hands of John H. Monn."[8]

Clyde Weyant was detained for the assault on Monn with a razor, but was later cleared of that charge. Perhaps Monn's 1913 foray with a razor, bolstered by the conflicting accounts of the incident, influenced the Commonwealth's decision to release Weyant.

Johns, Kniss, and Steckman were held under bail as material witnesses in the murder case. In addition, Burgess E. S. Myers suspended Johns from the police force pending the Monn case.

On the evening before the shooting, Molly Monn had told her husband that she was going to the show at the Arcade with some female friends. His remonstrated unsuccessfully against her going, so he went to the movies at the "It" theatre and returned home about ten o'clock. He then went to sleep on a couch in one of the dining rooms. Later testimony did reveal that Molly had instead attended the Arcade show with Clyde Weyant, who sat in the seat beside Molly.

At the coroner's inquest, Patrolman Johns testified that he saw Mrs. Monn on her way home from the Arcade around quarter till eleven. He went off his beat at quarter till one in the morning, and as he was entering his room at the boarding house, Mrs. Monn approached him and told him she was afraid to go to bed because of her husband. Johns volunteered to stay awake and watch over Molly. When Monn appeared, he, Molly, and Johns

---

[8] *Waynesboro Record*, March 6, 1918, p. 6, col. 4.

conversed for about an hour. John and Molly argued over John's refusal to buy tickets to the Arcade show, and Molly's asking Weyant to buy the tickets. After this exchange, Monn went downstairs, Molly went to bed, and Johns kept watch with his door open into the hall, opposite Molly's bedroom.

Later that morning, Johns testified, Monn came upstairs again, but upon seeing Johns on guard, he returned downstairs, where Johns could hear him making fires in the stoves. At five o'clock, Monn climbed the stairs a third time. Upon seeing Johns still on guard, he said, "Did you stay up all night ? Didn't need to, for I wasn't going to kill anyone." Thereupon Monn called Molly and returned downstairs. When Molly came out into the hall, she said to Johns, "I guess there will be trouble." Two minutes later, there was trouble in the form of a scream and a gunshot. And then a second shot. Johns went downstairs, opened the dining room door, saw Monn lying on the floor, and then found Molly in the kitchen. After Clyde Weyant joined him downstairs, the two boarders carried Mrs. Monn to a couch in the dining room. They ignored John Monn's requests for help.

Importantly, Johns testified that John Monn must have cut his throat between the time when he first saw Monn lying on the floor and when they laid Molly on the sofa, because his throat was not cut when Johns first investigated in the dining room. When Johns finally responded to John Monn's pleas for help, he noticed an open knife and a razor box lying on the floor near Monn but saw no razor.

Clyde Weyant testified that he had been boarding with the Monns since two weeks before Christmas. He admitted that he had purchased Molly's ticket to the Arcade show with the money she had given him for that purpose, but he bought his own ticket. He also admitted to occupying the seat beside her during the show. He noted that Molly was already at home when he returned at eleven o'clock. Then he and Monn talked briefly in his room, but Monn showed no anger towards him at that time. The gunshots roused him from sleep at half past five in the morning. When he heard them, he partly dressed and run downstairs.

Weyant admitted helping to carry Molly to the couch, but denied kissing her and threatening Monn. When asked why he declined to help Monn after the shooting, he stated that he felt that the one who had done the shooting deserved no help.

Dr. Croft testified that upon his arrival at the boarding house he found Monn lying on the floor in the room next the kitchen with one gash each in his throat and abdomen. His windpipe was severed, and he had difficulty communicating. He helped Monn to a couch, and washed his wounds but made no attempt to sew them up.

Dr. Croft found Molly lying dead on the sofa in the room in front of where John lay. Monn complained to Dr. Croft of the way his wife had been treating him for the past three weeks, and said he had decided to "end it all." He wrote on a piece of paper for the doctor to look under the couch where Molly lay. The doctor complied, and found a two and one-half page letter, presumably written by Monn. Molly had bled profusely, and her blood had run through the sofa onto the missive, making parts of it illegible. The essence of Monn's bloody epistle was as follows:

"Dear Mother—I wish you to take good care of Cletus and give him a good home and forgive me for all of this for I have seen plenty to cause this. It is on account of Clyde Weyant, Carl Steckman and Agnes Haugh made all of this trouble. I was treated like a dog for the last three weeks and last Wednesday I caught on to it and thought I would settle it all. Nobody knows what a life I had to bear in them three weeks so I thought I would settle it all and that would be the end of my trouble, so I want you all to forgive me. See that Cletus gets my gold watch. I hope God will forgive me and Mollie. I know she won't make no other man a fool or me no more this is the second time she has done this so I thought I would settle it all. Take care of my honey boy as long as you live for I can't stand it no longer. I have stood all I could so God bless all and goodbye all.

"Now Clyde you done all you could so I will settle all I no there wont be no more trouble through you no more. I thought you was a man but you see what it caused through you so I hope you can make trouble some where else where so I know you wont make it here no longer I will settle it all.

"Good-bye Cletus. That is what a bad man can do with a home so you all know the rest so good bye to all forgive J. H. M.

"Give my watch to Cletus and tell him good bye for pop * * * [obliterated by blood stains] this all so I will settle it all this is the second time she has done this so it will be the last time I will settle it all and I know I wont have no more trouble.

"Good bye Cletus, be a good boy for Big mom."[9]

With the assistance of Drs. D. M. Shoemaker and S. D. Shull, Dr. Croft performed an autopsy on the body of Molly Monn later that day. He found powder marks around her wound. He found the liver, stomach, bladder, and kidneys in normal condition. There was some shot through the large intestine, and arteries and veins were severed. Part of the pelvic bone was shot off. Death was bound to ensue within three or four minutes after the shooting, from hemorrhage. The body showed no other marks of a struggle.[10]

Molly Monn was buried in Price's Church graveyard (now Antietam Cemetery).[11]

When John Monn's mother visited him in the Chambersburg Hospital, he asked her to pray for him to die. His death seemed imminent, and he authorized J. R. Johns to dispose of his personal effects and household goods at public auction.[12] After his recovery became likely, however, Sheriff Enos Horst went to the hospital on March 20 and arrested Monn for Molly's murder. From that time until Monn's removal to jail on March 29, a guard stood watch over him.[13]

On Wednesday, April 24, 1918, John H. Monn pleaded not guilty to the charge of murder, and asked for a jury trial. The matter proceeded promptly to jury selection. Among the twelve men empanelled, Auctioneer A. D. Adams was the only Waynesboro resident. The *Waynesboro Record* observed—

> "It is hard to believe from the appearance of the accused man that he could have committed a crime so serious and revolting. By his action and appearance Monn showed evidence of refinement.

---

[9] *Waynesboro Record*, May 1, 1918, p. 6, col. 1.

[10] *Ibid.*

[11] Commonwealth of Pennsylvania Death Certificate #32734.

[12] "Wants to Die," *The Gettysburg Times* (Gettysburg, Pa.), March 8, 1913, p. 3.

[13] "In Bed, Seized for Murder," *The Evening News* (Harrisburg, Pa.), March 22, 1918, p. 13; "Wife Killer to Jail," *The Gettysburg Times*, March 30, 1918, p. 3.

He was neatly attired in a suit of dark fabric harmonizing perfectly with his slickly brushed black hair and carefully combed mustache.

"Around the neck of the prisoner, protruding from beneath an immaculate collar, was a bandage which concealed the long wound afflicted by a razor wielded, Monn has maintained, by Clyde Weyant, star boarder at the Monn home and alleged admirer of the murdered woman. Weyant, however, was exonerated from that accusation by the grand inquest.

"Monn conversed freely with his attorneys and rendered them much assistance in selecting the twelve men to decide his fate."[14]

After several hours of deliberation, those twelve men good and true found John Monn GUILTY OF VOLUNTARY MANSLAUGHTER, a crime which carried a maximum penalty of twelve years incarceration and a fine of one thousand dollars. Their decision came as quite a surprise to the small number of spectators gathered in the courtroom to hear the verdict, and the court did not deliver its customary commendation of the jury upon dismissing it. The prevailing opinion had been that the jury would find Monn guilty of second-degree murder.

The crowd had been much larger during the trial; in fact, it filled the courtroom. John Monn himself was the star witness. He testified dispassionately about Molly's alleged affairs with boarders Clyde Weyant, J. R. Johns, and Carl Steckman. He said that his wife had always become angry when he admonished her for "her evil ways." On one occasion she responded, "Go to h—. I'm running this ranch, not you."

Monn added that, about a week before the shooting, he had found Molly and Weyant together at the CG&W car barn, and his wife refused to return home with him until he threatened to summon the police.

The defendant further testified that, on the night before the shooting, he and his son, Cletus, had gone to the "It" theatre while Molly, Weyant, and Mr. and Mrs. Shindle attended the show at the Arcade. Monn arrived home first, and when he confronted Molly about her going to the show with Weyant, she remarked, "I don't want you to go with me any place, not even to a dog fight."

---

[14] *Waynesboro Record*, April 24, 1918, p. 1, col. 6.

Monn denied any intention of killing Molly. His story paralleled Patrolman Johns's version until the point where Molly went downstairs to prepare breakfast. Monn asserted that when he offered to help her fix breakfast, she replied, "I'll help *you* to get breakfast," and reached for Weyant's gun, which stood in the corner of the back dining room. During the ensuing tussle over the gun, he shot Molly. The gun kicked, Monn dropped it, and in some inexplicable way the gun discharged and the shot struck him. He could not explain how the strings on the gun trigger got there, but Chief of Police Gillan testified that they were there when he took possession of the gun at the Monn house.

Monn said that, when he regained consciousness, he asked J. R. Johns for a drink of water. Johns replied, "To h— with you," and passed on. Monn also denied seeing the note reading "Look under the couch" before it was produced as evidence at trial, and explained that the letter found under the couch referred not to his troubles with Molly but with his own health issues. He said that, in the end, he had concluded the best thing to do was to take Cletus and leave Molly. He added that Molly knew how to handle a gun better than he did, and that he had no idea how the shells had gotten into the gun or even where they had been kept.

"I had no idea of doing anything to that woman; I loved her too much."

On April 29, 1918, with "a blank countenance" John H. Monn heard the court sentence him to a term of no less than ten years nor more than twelve years in Eastern Penitentiary, a fine of one dollar, and court costs.[15]

Monn served his term of incarceration and returned to Franklin county, where he worked as a farm laborer. He died from congestive heart failure and senile arteriosclerosis in Waynesboro Hospital on December 15, 1960, and was buried in the Snow Hill graveyard, Quincy township.[16] His adopted son, Cletus, indeed went to live with his grandmother Monn after the shooting, and died July 3, 1980, in San Luis Obispo county, California.

---

[15] *Waynesboro Record*, May 1, 1918, p. 1, col. 4.
[16] Commonwealth of Pennsylvania Certificate of Death #114119-60.

X.
Miscellaneous Murders.

Todd Andrew Dorsett.

October 8, 2013.

The tenth meeting of the Potomac Street Irregulars was held at the Parlor House. Twenty-one persons attended. In default of an Irregular volunteering to present a case, the Moderator outlined some obscure homicide cases from early times.

BECAUSE the appetite of the Potomac Street Irregulars tends towards the digestion of murder cases, this presentation will outline a few of the homicides which have occurred hereabouts during the past two centuries. It is hoped that this summary will inspire other Irregulars to research these cases and engage the club at more length in the future with their respective analyses.

THE MURDER OF MRS. JOHN MCKEAN.

The earliest homicide in the Antietam country of which I could find mention was also one of the few Franklin county cases resulting in execution of the death penalty. In anticipation of an 1879 execution, newspapers revisited the various hangings which had occurred in Franklin county over the years:

> "The last execution in this county took place seventy-two years ago: On the 12th day of November, 1807, a man named John McKean was convicted of the murder of his wife, in Washington township, on the 30th of August previously, and was executed by Jacob Snyder, Sheriff of our county, on the 22d day of December, 1807—*Opinion*."[1]

---

[1] "Death Warrant," *The Village Record* (Waynesboro', Pa.), January 30, 1879, p. 2, col. 4.

THE SHOOTING OF JOHN OSBORNE.

Occasionally, the leading newspapers in America took notice of our local crimes. *The New York Times* mentioned the incident in which one or both of the sons of the late Tobias Funk killed the irascible shoemaker John Osborne:

> "PHILADELPHIA, Monday, Sept. 6.
> "A man named OSBORNE was shot dead near Waynesboro, Penn., yesterday by two brothers named DANIEL and DAVID FUNK, some dispute occurring between the three. OSBORNE was carrying water from the well belonging to the Funks at the time. Both of them have been arrested."[2]

The Waynesboro newspaper gave a more detailed account about Osborne's shooting:

> "*Unfortunate Affray—Man Shot and Mortally Wounded.*—On Sabbath evening last our community was started by the announcement that JOHN OSBORN, living near this place, by profession a shoemaker, had been shot, and it was thought, mortally wounded. It appears that he and his son went together to the spring for water, where they were assaulted by DANIEL and DAVID W. FUNK—David hitting the father with a stone, and Daniel firing a load of shot into his side, from the effects of which he died in the morning. The evidence of THOMAS OSBORN, son of the deceased, before the Jury of Inquest was in substance, we learn, as follows:—On Sunday evening about half an hour before sundown he and his father started for Daniel Funk's Spring, each carrying a bucket for the purpose of getting water—witness was slightly in advance of deceased. As they were emerging from the bushes near the Spring, the first thing to attract their attention was a stone whizzing past his head—a second stone also passed without doing any injury; but the third struck his father on the elbow, and the fourth on the back of the head, causing him to reel considerably, and whilst reeling Daniel shot, being at the time about 11 steps off. The deceased fell and Daniel Funk then kicked him several times. Witness further said that David W. Funk threw the stones. As soon as deceased was shot, that he (witness) ran to the road, holloed murder, &c. After a thorough examination of the body by Drs. BROTHERTON and HERING, the jury rendered a verdict

---

[2] "Fatal Affray," *The New York Times* (New York, N. Y.), September 7, 1858.

in accordance with the above facts. The parties previously, however, gave themselves up, and after a hearing before Justice STONER, were committed and sent to Chambersburg to await their trial.

"It may be well enough to state that this is but the one side of the unfortunate affair, and that rumors are in circulation in reference to previous difficulties and annoyances on the part of deceased's family, which will we presume develop themselves hereafter."[3]

The Funks were tried for the murder of John Osborne. The account of their ordeal filled the entire front page of *The Village Record* and part of the second page. The surviving record of this incident is sufficient to warrant a more detailed Potomac Street Irregulars analysis.

THE MURDER OF JOHN S. HOLLINGER.

On June 1, 1885, Daniel Hollinger and his twenty-seven-year-old son, John S. Hollinger, were aroused by the barking of their watchdog at their farm near Roadside. The father did not leave the yard, but the son went into or near the barn, where he found several thieves. Someone shot John, and he was later found dead behind the barn, his breast pierced by a bullet. Approximately eight shots were fired, and it was not known whether John hit any of the intruders.[4]

The shooting of John S. Hollinger is one of the unsolved mysteries in Antietam History. Eight years afterwards, at the time Emanuel Monn was murdered, the authorities speculated whether the same persons were involved in both crimes. In the eighteen-eighties and early –nineties, Henry Heist, who was hanged for the Monn murder, was one of the best known chicken thieves in the neighbourhood of Glen Forney and Roadside.

THE HANGING OF HENRY HEIST.

Although technically a solved case, the murder of Emanuel Monn, which the Irregulars discussed in summary during our inaugural meeting, still excites debate among local residents. The controversy surrounding the case arises from the fact that a man

[3] *The Village Record*, September 9, 1858, p. 2, col. 1.
[4] *The Village Record*, June 4, 1885 p. 2, col. 3.

protesting his innocence was convicted and hanged based solely on circumstantial evidence. *The New York Times* deemed the
case newsworthy:

"GETTYSBURG, Pa., Jan. 17.—Henry Heist was hanged here this
morning. He murdered Emanuel Monn. Heist and Monn were
woodchoppers, living in a small cabin the mountains west of this
place. The theory of the Commonwealth as to the motive for the
crime was that Heist was jealous of the attentions of Monn to a
disreputable woman. The evidence was entirely circumstantial."[5]

THE SHOOTING OF JOHN JOHNSTON.

At the Glendale siding on the railroad north of Waynecastle, an
argument between boss and worker ended in a fatal shooting on
July 17, 1901. The brother of the contractor working on the siding, J. G. Howie, of Monroe, North Carolina, argued with a laborer, John Johnston, and shot at him twice. Johnston became angry because Howie had called him early in the morning to start
work. Perhaps racially motivated, Howie resented Johnston's
tone, and after an argument, shot Johnston, killing him. Johnston was buried in potter's field, and Howie escaped.[6]

THE BARNES–DAYWALT GUNFIGHT.[7]

Abram and William Barnes, of Glen Forney, were downtown in
Waynesboro using vile language and goading Waynesboro Police
Officer D. William Daywalt, who followed them and attempted
to arrest them in Alley No. 1 North. This action resulted in a gun
battle in the east end of town in which a little girl was shot in
the leg, and several other citizens narrowly escaped being shot.
The streets were crowded with people returning home from the
Biederwolf revival meeting. Daywalt and Chief of Police S. W.
Staley pursued the Barnes brothers out the Roadside road. "Abe"
Barnes shot Daywalt, and as the latter lay dying in a wheat field

---

[5] *The New York Times*, January 18, 1894.

[6] *Waynesboro Record* (Waynesboro, Pa.), July 18, 1901.

[7] During 2014, PSI Amy Fleagle Dennis adopted this case and made a thorough
investigation. Her PowerPoint presentation about it was the first of its kind at
a PSI meeting.

belonging to Edward Hess (now Meadowbrook), the Barneses were in the distance shouting with glee over shooting him. Chief Staley came to Daywalt's aid, but the officer soon expired near where he fell. He left a wife and five children. A State policeman shot and killed Abe Barnes the next morning, and "Bill" Barnes, the younger brother, then surrendered.[8]

THE SHOOTING OF ELLSWORTH CARBAUGH.

Much mystery surrounded the shooting of Ellsworth Carbaugh because there was no apparent reason, or motive, for it. A jury found Abram Fitz, of Waynesboro, guilty of murder in the second degree, but Fitz protested that he knew not how the gun used in the shooting got out of his suitcase where it had been kept for eleven years. Carbaugh died at Waynesboro Hospital. Judge Watson R. Davison sentenced Fitz to eight to sixteen years' imprisonment in Eastern Penitentiary.[9]

---

[8] *Waynesboro Record*, February 4, 1914.
[9] *The Record Herald* (Waynesboro, Pa.), November 29, 1933.

OLD FRANKLIN COUNTY JAIL,
erected in 1818.

XI.
The Murder of Sadie Hurley Mathna.

Sue Lee.

November 12, 2013.

The eleventh meeting of the Potomac Street Irregulars was held at the Parlor House with twenty-six persons in attendance. PSI Sue Lee researched the Mathna murder and William Reed's execution so thoroughly, and discussed the case so articulately, that the group was at a loss to ask questions.*

ON the morning of May 9, 1911, tucked away on the edge of Pennsylvania's southernmost forest lands, Miss Sarah Conklin, matron, was working in the garden of the Mont Alto Forestry Academy. It was about nine o'clock when she saw forty-one-year-old William F. Reed coming up the lawn toward the house. He entered the kitchen through the rear door.

Miss Margaret Bricker, a domestic servant, left the kitchen as Reed entered. She was going outside to buy bread from George Miley, the Mont Alto baker. A short while later three shots along with screams were heard coming from the kitchen.

Reed came out of the rear kitchen door, shoving a revolver into his pocket. He walked past Miley and said, "I fixed her this time."

Miss Conklin, who was still in the garden, saw Reed come out of the kitchen with a revolver in his hand. He placed it in his right hip pocket as he descended the porch. She then ran into the kitchen and found the room filled with smoke. A coffee grinder was on the floor with its top broken, a large can of coffee was overturned, and a picture was on the table with a ball of cord beside it. The pantry door was ajar, and smoke filled that

---

*Mrs. Lee drew information from the following sources: *The Public Opinion* (Chambersburg, Pa.) and *The Gettysburg Times* (Gettysburg, Pa.); Ancestry.com; and materials deposited in the Franklin County Library, Chambersburg, Pa., and the campus library and Wiestling Hall, Mont Alto Campus of the Pennsylvania State University.

room as well. Miss Conklin frantically began to look for domestic worker Sadie (Hurley) Mathna. When she could not find her in the kitchen or the pantry, she ran up the back stairs to check in her bedroom. Not finding her, she returned to the first floor and entered the dining room. There she found the twenty-nine-year-old Mrs. Mathna near death, lying in the southwest corner of the room. She was lying on her right side with her face toward the wall. Margaret Bricker, hearing the shots, then joined Miss Conklin in the dining room.

John Shaffer and Harry Mentzer, who had heard the shots as well, entered the dining room and carried a barely alive Sadie up the back stairs and laid her on a sofa. She was not conscious and gave only a few moans before her death.

Professor H. L. Zeigler, superintendent of the academy, was at the stables with a man named Patterson harnessing a horse when they heard the shots. Knowing that someone must have been shot, Zeigler immediately called the police and a physician. The men then ran toward the house. They passed Reed going westward, and gave his description to the police.

Reed walked into Mont Alto and encountered Romaine Small on the street and said, "Well she's dead. I've shot Sadie and I am going to give myself up." Then he walked on to the magistrate's office, where he surrendered to his uncle Constable Jacob Wile.

>>>>>>>>●<<<<<<<

William F. Reed was born September 21, 1869, the son of William H. Reed and his wife, *nee* Rebecca Wile. He worked as a laborer, and enlisted in the army on May 28, 1896.

Sarah C. Hurley was born February 14, 1881, at Roxbury, Franklin county. She was the daughter of Jacob H. Hurley and his wife, *nee* Elizabeth Doughterman. "Sadie" was baptized on February 20, 1893. On June 10, 1898, at Hagerstown, Maryland, she married Reuben Mathna (1877–1940). She bore him one child, Della Mae Mathna (Mrs. John Sheller Benedict; 1900–1992). Sadie was estranged from Mathna at the time of her death.

Sarah "Sadie" Hurley Mathna and William F. Reed met in 1908, when Sadie was living and working at the academy. In late September 1909, she left to keep house for Reed on North Franklin street, Waynesboro. In May 1910 they moved to a tenant house owned by Bruce Cale but stayed there only until August of the same year. Thereupon Miss Hurley moved to Chambersburg to live with her mother. It is unknown where Reed then resided, but the couple continued to spend time together at Chambersburg every Saturday and Sunday evening.

On November 28, 1910, the Forestry Academy rehired Sadie, and she moved into quarters there. Reed continued to call on her but was getting agitated because he wanted her to move back in with him, which she refused to do. On many occasions, he was heard making threats against her.

A neighbor of Miss Hurley's mother, William Robinson, said he and Mr. Reed were talking one day and Sadie called out to him. Reed remarked, "I am going to kill that woman yet." Robinson advised him to leave her alone, and Reed replied, "If I had thirty cents I would go to Waynesboro to get a gun. She is not true to me or the man hanging around her."

In March 1911, Reed called on Sadie at the academy, but Miss Conklin told him that Sadie was not at home. Reed retorted, "That woman will fool around until I kill her." Miss Conklin responded, "You have no claim to Sadie." Reed then said, "I have been mighty good to her." Later, when asked why she had not reported the threat, Miss Conklin said she felt it unwise to interfere in others' affairs. She did, however, warn Sadie to be careful around him.

On another occasion, Reed saw Samuel Mines across from the Leland hotel and asked him, "Did you see my girl?" Mines replied that he had, and Reed said, "She'll be damn sorry when I go up there."

On the days leading up to the murder, Reed had been in Ohio with Romaine Small. He returned to Waynesboro on Friday, May 5, 1911. He and Small had returned earlier than expected because Small was so disgusted with the way Reed was acting. Small said that Reed was totally different from ever before. There was something wrong with him: all he did was walk about all of the time.

Once back at Waynesboro, he stayed Saturday and Sunday night in the home of his sister and brother-in-law Emily and Sam Rook. Mrs. Rook said that Reed's mind was in very bad condition. Reed told her to wash and dry his clothes and then throw them away. He then threw his hat on the floor and told a boy to tramp on it. Mrs. Rook said that Reed also paced the floor crying, "My God, my head. I am crazy."

At some point on Sunday, Reed went to the Forestry Academy to visit Sadie, but she was not at home. She had been seen around Mont Alto with a man named Jacob McFadden. This fueled Reed's anger. He asked his brother-in-law if he knew where he could get a gun. Sam said that he was acting very strange, so he told Reed he could not get one. Reed then asked Irvin Martz if he could get one. Martz said that he thought he could get one by Monday morning. Martz borrowed a .38-calibre revolver from Guy Rowe and gave it to Reed around six o'clock Monday evening.

Prior to obtaining the gun, Reed had gone to the Washington Café, Waynesboro, where the bar clerk refused to sell him liquor because he appeared to have already had too much to drink.

A neighbor of the Rooks', Mrs. Mary Wingert, said that she had seen Reed around two o'clock to four o'clock Monday afternoon, rolling around on the porch moaning and holding his head.

Later Monday evening, Reed went to the residence of his brother and sister-in-law George and Mary Reed for dinner. He was acting very strange, and Mary was afraid to be in the same room with him. George Reed said William seemed to be out of his mind and very drunk, so he ordered him out of the house.

Mrs. Wingert again saw William Reed on Tuesday morning around half past seven. She stated that Reed said "Good morning" to her but still appeared very drunk.

Reed was also seen on the Tuesday morning train to Mont Alto. Joseph Monn said he spoke to Reed, who appeared to be calm and sober. Once off the train, Reed walked to the academy grounds, where he saw John Shaffer and asked if Sadie was in the kitchen. Shaffer told him that she was.

Inside the kitchen, Reed asked Sadie for some things of his which she had taken out of a chest which belonged to him: a picture of him in the army, his discharge papers, and some old letters. She refused, and they quarrelled. Finally Sadie jumped up and said, "All right, I'll get them." She returned to the kitchen, walked around the table, and threw the items in the range. Reed said that he would slap her for putting his papers in the fire. Sadie told him that if he did not leave she would knock his head off. She then raised the coffee grinder and threw up her other arm to strike him. Reed then pulled his gun, threw up his arm to protect himself from the grinder, and fired. He stated that he fired only to scare her. He fired three times. All three bullets hit Sadie: one entered the left side of her face, one entered her left side and was embedded in the right side of her back, and one entered her chest and passed through her heart and caused her death.

Sadie staggered from the kitchen into the dining room, leaving a trail of blood. Weak and stunned from the wounds, she retained enough strength to make an effort to escape the man who sought her life. When she reached the dining room, she fell to the floor.

When asked why he had borrowed the revolver, Reed replied that he had wanted to go to Tomstown, and was afraid to go without a gun. He never made it to Tomstown, however, because he got the revolver too late to go.

Reed Pleads Insanity.

William F. Reed was indicted for first-degree murder. His trial began on September 7, 1911. Reed's legal counsel, Messrs. Hoke and Elder, argued that Reed had a brain storm and that his mind was inflamed by alcohol when he shot Sadie. On Saturday, September 9, at 4:42 P.M., the jury began its deliberations, which lasted twenty-eight hours. They cast fourteen ballots before they reached a verdict of GUILTY OF MURDER IN THE FIRST DEGREE.

Reed remained calm, and showed no emotion when the court read the sentence of death. While awaiting his fate in the Franklin County Jail, Chambersburg, Reed passed time by reading and attending Sunday church services. At times he was despondent.

On the morning of April 30, 1912, with the same remarkable nerve of which he gave evidence throughout his trial and his days in prison, William F. Reed walked firmly across the platform to the scaffold and did not flinch when his eyes fell on the gallows. He gave the attending officials no trouble. Deputy Sheriff Kuhn bound Reed's ankles while Sheriff Walker drew the black hood over Reed's head and adjusted the noose. Reed remained silent and motionless. Without pause, the sheriff turned to the lever and gave it a quick tug, and the gallows of Franklin county fell for the last time.[1]

---

[1] The official causes of Reed's death, from "legal execution," were "hanging" and "fractured cervical vertebra." Commonwealth of Pennsylvania Certificate of Death #34596.

A HANGING.

XII.
Holiday Murder Mystery Dinner.

December 10, 2013.

WENTY-FOUR persons attended the twelfth meeting of the Potomac Street Irregulars, held at "History House," residence of T. A. Dorsett, Waynesboro. Following a social hour, guests enjoyed a dinner of pork roast, vegetables, and ice cream. The after-dinner entertainment consisted of the play of two murder mystery games, one in each dining room. Miss Kimberly Zajac assisted Moderator Dorsett in catering the dinner, and Mrs. Bruce Katzmann loaned PSI several murder mystery kits for the party.

Anyone who had attended at least two PSI meetings during the year qualified to attend the event. The following dined at President Rock's table: Mr. and Mrs. Allen M. Baumgardner, Mr. and Mrs. Frank Bock, Mr. and Mrs. Harry G. Morningstar, Mr. and Mrs. F. Marshall Rock, and Mr. and Mrs. Fred S. White. Moderator Dorsett hosted the room's game. Mesdames Bock and White solved the mystery.

Those dining at Miss Shirley A. Zeigler's table were Mrs. Sue Lee, Mr. and Mrs. J. Michael Logan, Mr. Rick Mummert, Mrs. Crystal Emory Payne, Mr. and Mrs. Michael Pecotte, Mrs. Julie Shifflett, Mrs. Lori Shindledecker, Mr. Frank Shockey, Mrs. Darlene Shockey Weddle, and Miss Zeigler. Mrs. Stephen L. Monn hosted the room's game, and Mr. Shockey solved the mystery.

At the conclusion of the games, prizes were awarded. PSI Frank Bock won the popular vote for the best presentation in 2013. His investigation into the Kennedy murder easily surpassed all others in popularity and attendance. His prize was a vintage Armatale plate depicting the Buena Vista Spring Hotel, where, coincidentally, he had worked during its reincarnation as Bellarmine Hall.

PSIs Barbara Bock, Darlene Shockey Weddle, Frank Shockey,

and T. A. Dorsett received gifts of Antietam Historical Association merchandise for perfect attendance during the year.

Winners of the murder mystery games received gift boxes of candy from Zoe's Chocolates, Waynesboro.

Everyone seemed to enjoy a festive conclusion to a happy and successful first year of Potomac Street Irregulars proceedings.

SUBSCRIBERS.

Mr. Malcolm B. Angle
Mr. H. Wayne Bartholow
Mr. and Mrs. Allen Baumgardner
John E. N. Blair, J.D.
Frank & Barbara Bock
Shelley Bracken
Shirley Eva Brown
Pat Cadwell
Mr. William D. Calhoun
Mr. Roger J. Causse
Mr. Brian Churchill
Mr. David E. Cline
Rose Cline
Jo Ellen Crider
Mrs. Dan H. Dietrich
Todd Andrew Dorsett
Judith F. Elden
Jon and Linda Fleagle
Dawn E. Garner
Dan & MaryAnne Haffner
Gene Helman
Linda Higginbotham
Marthaann Hollinger
Mr. Aldus R. Hoover
Mr. Richard Lee Hovis
Mr. Jim Huff
Mr. and Mrs. Gary Johnson
Mr. Michael D. Kauffman
Mr. Dale O. Kennedy
George and Dottie Kirk
Mary B. Kline
Mrs. Sue Lee
Larry and Jeanine Ludy, Jr.

Susan McCleaf Lyons
Sally Yingst Manning
Tammy McCardell
Mr. Jeffrey L. McLaughlin, Sr.
Julie Shockey Meminger
Mr. Jeff Mentzer
Elaine Merletti
Harry & Louise Morningstar
Mr. Butch Murdorf
Mr. Scott K. Parker
Michael & Sarah Pecotte
Tim & Nancy Redding
Cathy Roberts
Mr. and Mrs. F. Marshall Rock
Earle and Dixie Rook
Mr. Michael Rook
Barbara Samsell
Mark & Brenda Scriptunas
Lori Shindledecker
Mr. Brian J. Shockey
Mr. Danny Shockey
Mr. Franklin J. Shockey
Mr. Tim Shockey
Deborah Shull Sirk
Barbara Smith
Sally T. Stanley/Kevin M. Bilder
Sue Stoner
Mr. and Mrs. Michael J. Toms
Patricia Tresler
Darlene Shockey Weddle
Edna M. Zeigler
Miss Shirley A. Zeigler
Mr. Maurice E. Zimmerman

INDEX.

Case Notes.

Case Notes.

Case Notes.

Case Notes.

Case Notes.

Case Notes.

Case Notes.